ENDORSEMENTS

"At the heart of all true spiritual vitality is a prioritization of knowing God. The Cappadocian Fathers, as they defended the deity of the Son and the Holy Spirit in all of their Triune glory, knew this as they emphasized the infinitude of God. Their younger contemporary Augustine was gripped by it as he sought to respond to the fundamental error that the human will is powerful enough to lay hold of God's salvific mercy by itself. John Wycliffe was ever conscious of the perfect moral excellence of God as he critiqued the institutional church of his day. Martin Luther, Hugh Latimer, and John Calvin were similarly in awe of the greatness of their God and overwhelmed by His lovingkindness as they stood fast for the gospel in the sixteenth century. And in that iconic age of revivals, the long eighteenth century, Jonathan Edwards and Andrew Fuller were motivated by the glory of God as the *telos* of all creation as they preached and wrote for their day. In like fashion, this small volume by Steve Lawson confronts our generation with this great truth of the glory of God in all of His divine attributes. Must reading for a man-centered day!"

—Dr. Michael A.G. Haykin
Chair and professor of church history,
the Southern Baptist Theological Seminary
Louisville, Ky.

"The longer I live, the clearer it becomes to me that unless one begins with the true knowledge of God, nothing else in the world, in life, or in the Christian life makes any sense at all. Those who begin below, with circumstances, and attempt to reason up, drawing conclusions about God (that He is kind or cruel, accessible or aloof, powerful or weak) inevitably err. Only as we begin with the truth of God (that He is sovereign, almighty, wise, good, and just) and reason down to our circumstances (be they good or bad), does life begin to make sense. Steve Lawson has provided us with a comprehensive survey of the attributes of the God of the Bible. His twenty chapters of roughly six pages each can easily be incorporated into one's morning devotions, providing his readers with a satisfying diet of biblical insight into the God of whom to know is life eternal (John 17:3)."

—Dr. Terry Johnson
Senior minister, Independent Presbyterian Church
Savannah, Ga.

"On the eve of His crucifixion Jesus prayed that God, the Holy Trinity, would be glorified through the cross. He then added, 'This is eternal life, that they know you, the only true God, and Jesus Christ whom you have sent' (John 17:3). Our experience and enjoyment of eternal life, as well as our progress in the life of faith are inseparably bound up with knowing God and bringing Him honor. Dr. Lawson, with a pastor-teacher's heart and skill, takes us by the hand in this volume and brings us face-to-face with God as He has revealed Himself in the Bible and supremely in His Son, Christ Jesus. In so doing, he will surely bring some to know and love God for the first time, others to know Him better, and all to be filled with worship, love, and praise for the One who alone can make us whole."

—Rev. Mark G. Johnston
Minister, Bethel Presbyterian Church
Cardiff, Wales

Show Me Your Glory

SHOW
ME
YOUR
GLORY

UNDERSTANDING *the*
MAJESTIC SPLENDOR
of GOD

STEVEN J. LAWSON

 LIGONIER MINISTRIES

Show Me Your Glory: Understanding the Majestic Splendor of God
© 2020 by Steven J. Lawson

Published by Ligonier Ministries
421 Ligonier Court, Sanford, FL 32771
Ligonier.org

Printed in York, Pennsylvania
Maple Press
0000721
First edition, second printing

ISBN 978-1-64289-263-5 (Hardcover)
ISBN 978-1-64289-264-2 (ePub)
ISBN 978-1-64289-265-9 (Kindle)

Cover design: Ligonier Creative
Interior design and typeset: Katherine Lloyd, The DESK

Scripture quotations are taken from the New American Standard Bible® (NASB), Copyright © 1960, 1962, 1963, 1968, 1971, 1972, 1973, 1975, 1977, 1995 by The Lockman Foundation. Used by permission. www.Lockman.org

The Library of Congress has cataloged the Reformation Trust edition as follows:

Names: Lawson, Steven J., author.
Title: Show me your glory : understanding the majestic splendor of God / Steven J. Lawson.
Description: First edition. | Sanford, FL : Reformation Trust Publishing, a division of Ligonier Ministries, Orlando, FL, 2020. | Includes index.
Identifiers: LCCN 2019058935 (print) | LCCN 2019058936 (ebook) | ISBN 9781642892635 (hardback) | ISBN 9781642892642 (epub) | ISBN 9781642892659 (kindle edition)
Subjects: LCSH: God (Christianity)--Attributes.
Classification: LCC BT130 .L35 2020 (print) | LCC BT130 (ebook) | DDC 231/.4--dc23
LC record available at https://lccn.loc.gov/2019058935
LC ebook record available at https://lccn.loc.gov/2019058936

This book is dedicated to:

John and Dori Anderson

I give thanks to God for these dear and faithful friends,
who have been like family to our family.
Their love and friendship have meant the world to me,
which has greatly encouraged me through the
many years.

CONTENTS

HIGHER
GROUND

I will never forget when I first became aware of the attributes of God.

As a young seminary student, I walked into the campus bookstore to browse through the books on the shelves. One particular book spine caught my attention, and like a proverbial moth to the flame, I was drawn to pick it up.

The book was *A Body of Divinity* by Thomas Watson. Curious about Watson, I read the book's dust jacket and found out that he was a Puritan who lived in seventeenth-century England. This intriguing book, I learned, contained his sermons on the Westminster Shorter Catechism.

I turned to the table of contents, and I was amazed to discover that the entire first page listed chapters about God. There was more of God in the table of contents alone than there was in many contemporary Christian books I had seen. In fact, the largest section of the two-page table of contents dealt exclusively with God Himself.

The table of contents listed individual chapters on the being and knowledge of God. It followed with chapters on the attributes of God: the eternality, unchangeableness, wisdom, power, holiness, justice, mercy, and truth of God. The book also touched on the unity, Trinity, and providence of God. The whole rest of the book flowed out of this profound teaching on God.

This was the first time in my life that I had seen a list of the attributes of God. I was immediately captivated by the theocentric emphasis of this book. Impulsively, I bought the book and took it home with me, little realizing the impact it would have on my life.

As I read *A Body of Divinity*, my view of God became bigger and bigger with every page. New categories of thinking about God were being planted in my mind. My heart was being deepened. My theology was being dramatically elevated. My worldview was being expanded. My Christian life was being steered in a radically different direction, toward higher ground.

What made the difference? I was seeing God for who He is. The attributes of God so clearly revealed His holy character that my life would never be the same again.

This book, *Show Me Your Glory*, is a humble attempt to set before you these same attributes of God that so revolutionized my life. My desire is that these same transcendent truths will significantly shape your life into who you must become. May you never see God the same way again, and may you therefore never see yourself, your salvation, or the world in which you live the same way again.

Blessings in Christ,
Steven J. Lawson
Dallas

Chapter One

MAJESTICALLY AWESOME

The Glory of God I

I think the greatest weakness in our day is the virtual eclipse of the character of God, even within our churches.

—R.C. Sproul

In the early years of Ligonier Ministries, when its outreach began to blossom and expand, a consultant was brought in to meet with its founder, Dr. R.C. Sproul. The goal was to develop a vision and strategy for this rapidly growing ministry. In the initial phase, the consultant asked Dr. Sproul two diagnostic questions. The first was this: "What is the greatest need of people in the world?" Without hesitation, Dr. Sproul answered, "People in the world need to know who God is."

Probing deeper to better understand the focus of the ministry, the consultant then asked, "What is the greatest need of people in the church?" Dr. Sproul again answered without hesitation: "People in the church need to know who God is."

Dr. Sproul was right. The greatest need of every individual is to know who God is. No matter who a person is—whether he is inside the church or outside of it, whether he is a true believer or a militant atheist—his most basic need is to know God if he is to know himself and understand the world around him. He must know who God is and what He is like. Every other knowledge that someone may acquire is a far distant second in importance. Everything in an individual's life is affected by his knowledge of God. A true knowledge of what He is like is *that* important.

NOTHING MORE IMPORTANT

The most important aspect of who we are is what comes into our minds when we think of God. The trajectory of our lives is directed by our understanding of God. Moreover, our eternal destiny hinges on our relationship to Him and who we believe He is. If we are to live as He intends us to live, we must know who He is and what He is like.

As our knowledge of God goes, so goes the direction of our lives. A high view of God will lead us to lofty worship of Him. A growing understanding of His character will lead to holy and righteous living in the pursuit of His will. Conversely, a low view of God will lead to diminished praise of Him. Inevitably, base views of Him will lead to low and empty living.

There is nothing more important in our lives than knowing God and living for the glory of His great and awesome name.

The apostle Paul wrote, "Whether, then, you eat or drink or whatever you do, do all to the glory of God" (1 Cor. 10:31). Living for God's glory must permeate every part of our lives—as we wake up in the morning, as we go to work, as we attend school, as we worship in church, as we serve the Lord, and as we go to sleep at night. Twenty-four hours a day, seven days a week, every moment is to be lived for the glory of God.

THE FIRMEST FOUNDATION

Knowing God and beholding His glory is foundational to everything in our lives. To build on any other footing is to build on shifting sand. Either we live for the glory of God, or we do not live at all—we only exist. If we are to truly live as He intends, our hearts must be, first and foremost, directed toward the pursuit of God's glory. God's glory must be primary and all else a far distant second. To fail to live for the glory of God is to endure an empty existence. God must be the epicenter of our lives. We exist for His glory—God created us for this high purpose. This must be our chief end. Otherwise, we have squandered our lives.

Living for the glory of God is the beginning and end of all things. This divine glory is the blazing sun around which our lives must revolve. When we come to the end of our lives, all that will matter is an affirmative answer to this crucial question: Did we live for the glory of God? If we fail to live for God, we have wasted our lives upon the earth. But if we seek God's glory, our lives will have been well spent and lived to the fullest. Only in the pursuit of the glory of God will our lives count for time and eternity.

ONE COMPELLING PASSION

To best grasp this ultimate priority, I want us to consider a man who lived more than three thousand years ago for the glory of God. He stands as a timeless example of a life lived for God, and he is just as relevant today as when he first pursued God. This man was Moses, who led the exodus of the nation of Israel out of Egyptian bondage. He was the author of the first five books in the Bible—Genesis through Deuteronomy. Here is a man who dared to cry out to God, "Show me Your glory!" (Ex. 33:18). Here is a man living in the passionate pursuit of God's glory. Here is a man sold out to know more of the glory of God. This driving ambition of his life is an example for each of us and is worthy of our emulation.

Here is the background for this dramatic encounter that Moses had with God. The place is Mount Sinai, and Moses has already been to the mountaintop once. While Moses was meeting with God on the summit to receive the law, the people were down in the valley breaking His law by crafting an idol to worship. When he came down and saw what the people were doing, Moses, in righteous indignation, smashed the two tablets containing the inscription of the Ten Commandments. Leading these wayward people on this journey to the promised land would prove to be the greatest challenge of his life.

AN EARNEST PRAYER

If there was ever a man who needed to know more of God, it was Moses. If there was ever a time for this increased knowledge, it was now. How could he bear up under such demanding difficulties? How could he persevere under such distressing adversity? How could this man of God endure through the enormous challenges of leading millions of rebellious Israelites? The answer is simple, yet profound. He needed a deeper knowledge of God.

The same is true for each one of us. If we are to live life to the fullest, we must know the God who has made us in His image. If we are to meet the many difficulties before us, we must know Him who has an eternal purpose and plan for our lives. Otherwise, we will be reduced to a mundane life that misses the mark He has designed for us.

GOD IS GLORIOUS

The request Moses made that momentous day was extraordinarily daring: "I pray You, show me Your glory!" (Ex. 33:18). When he offered this audacious prayer, he had already seen the glory of God in ways that far exceeded what anyone else had beheld of the glory of God.

Before this encounter with God, Moses had already stood on holy ground at the burning bush. He had heard the audible voice of God say, "I AM WHO I AM" (Ex. 3:14). At the time of this daring request, Moses had already witnessed the pillar of cloud lead Israel out of Egypt (Ex. 13). He had seen the invisible hand of God part the Red Sea and drown Pharaoh's hordes (Ex. 14). He had already seen water come gushing out of a rock (Ex. 17) and had beheld the fire fall on Mount Sinai and consume the mountainside (Ex. 19). Moses had already glimpsed these manifestations of the glory of God. Yet Moses still prays, "Show me Your glory!"

Moses is praying that he would see and experience a yet deeper knowledge of God. Moses understood he had only skimmed the surface of the bottomless depths of the majesty of God. He had barely placed the tip of his smallest finger into the vast oceans of the wonders of God. He must know *more* of this awesome God.

THE WEIGHT OF GREATNESS

When Moses prayed for an increased knowledge of God's glory, we must understand the meaning of this word *glory*. It translates a

Hebrew word (*kabod*) that means "heavy" or "weight." In ancient times, the greatness of a man was determined by the weight of his assets. The richer the man was, the weightier was the accumulation of his silver, gold, and precious jewels. The word represented the greatness of a man in his surrounding community. The weight of his wealth determined the measure of the influence he had.

As related to God, the word *glory* represents the infinite weightiness of who He is. The glory of God reflects the sum and substance of His holy character. It encompasses His divine perfections, attributes, and essence. It includes His holiness, sovereignty, righteousness, omnipotence, omniscience, omnipresence, truth, grace, mercy, goodness, love, and wrath. It is the godness of God. In short, the glory of God is the display of His infinite grandeur and vast greatness.

This prayer that God would reveal more of His greatness is what Moses must experience to find the strength to persevere. After leaving Egypt and coming to Mount Sinai, Moses is confronted with the mounting challenges of his ministry. He is facing the pressures of leading a group of rebellious Israelites through the wilderness. With an expanded knowledge of God, he can withstand any difficulty in the long journey that lay ahead. With a more intimate knowledge of God, he can persevere through the toughest times. If God will show him His glory, he can endure the fiery trials and afflictions that are to come.

GOD IS SELF-REVEALING

God chooses to respond to Moses' request with an affirmative statement. God said, "I Myself will make all My goodness pass before you, and will proclaim the name of the LORD before you;

and I will be gracious to whom I will be gracious, and will show compassion on whom I will show compassion" (Ex. 33:19). God answered positively, indicating He would make His glory known to Moses in yet greater ways. When we come to God in humble submission, desiring to know more of Him, He delights to reveal more of Himself to us.

God says, "I Myself will make all My goodness pass before you." In this passage, God's glory is equated with His goodness. This aspect of God represents His moral purity. God added that He "will proclaim the name of the LORD before you" (v. 19). This means He will preach to Moses and expound His own glory. The word "proclaim" (Hebrew *qara*) carries the idea of raising one's voice and declaring. It is sometimes used to describe the roaring of a lion. God announces that He will bring an authoritative and powerful exposition of Himself to Moses. This will be a fervent and passionate proclamation by God to His servant. Specifically, God will preach on "the name of the LORD." The divine name refers to everything that God is—the whole of His nature, character, and person.

Moses can only know God to the extent that God chooses to make Himself known. The greater must condescend to the lesser. Moses can make no demands on God. Moses can only appeal to God to reveal more of Himself. This self-revelation of God is entirely at His sovereign discretion.

Likewise, each one of us can only know God to the measure that He allows us to know Him. Some of us will be more intimate with God than others. Some of us will pursue Him more than others. But each one of us must pursue Him with eagerness, knowing He rewards those who seek Him (Heb. 11:6).

GOD IS AUTONOMOUS

At the heart of what God chooses to proclaim to Moses is the truth of His sovereign grace and saving mercy. God says, "I will be gracious to whom I will be gracious." This graciousness toward undeserving, sinful creatures is the apex of His glory. He will sovereignly choose to set His saving favor on whomever He will. In other words, God will deal with Moses in mercy, unlike the exercise of His wrath toward Pharaoh and the Egyptians.

God is autonomous. He will do whatever He pleases. He alone possesses the right of self-government and has complete freedom in His actions. God is self-ruling and self-determining. He is independent of the will of His creatures, both sovereign and free in His actions.

If you want to understand the glory of God, understand this statement: "I will be gracious to whom I will be gracious." The apostle Paul quotes this verse at the very apex of his argument in Romans 9, teaching the freedom of the divine will: "I will have mercy on whom I have mercy, and I will have compassion on whom I have compassion" (v. 15). Then Paul explains, "So then He has mercy on whom He desires, and He hardens whom He desires" (v. 18). To behold God's glory to a greater extent is to perceive more carefully His electing grace and predestinating mercy. This divine disclosure is taking Moses deeper into the heart of God.

The mercy of God is His tenderhearted compassion for those who are helpless and hopeless in their sin. In a step of unmerited favor, God, who is "rich in mercy" (Eph. 2:4), chooses to draw near to those who are ruined by their iniquities. The apostle Paul writes, "He saved us, not on the basis of deeds which we have done in righteousness, but according to His mercy" (Titus 3:5). It is His mercy that moves Him to save those who are perishing. Peter notes, "Blessed be the God and Father of our Lord Jesus Christ, who according to His great mercy has caused us to be born again to a living hope" (1 Peter 1:3). To understand the greatness of God's glory is to understand that He sets His heart on sinners whom He has chosen to save. He sees us in our state of utter ruin. For reasons known only to God, He chooses to have mercy on those who have no claim to it.

Has God in Christ set His mercy on you? Has God chosen to have compassion on you? If so, this is an extraordinary unveiling of His glory toward you.

GOD IS AWESOME

If Moses is to behold this greater display of divine glory, God must mercifully set restrictions on His self-revelation. If God manifested all that He is in His blazing glory, Moses would immediately die. He could not withstand beholding the full revelation of the glory of God. Finite flesh cannot look on an infinite God and live. It would be easier for Moses to look directly into the blazing light of the sun than to look on God in His dazzling glory. Therefore, God graciously gave Moses these constraints so he would not die.

God then explained why these restrictions were necessary: "You cannot see My face, for no man can see Me and live!" (Ex. 33:20). Such a close encounter with God would strike Moses dead. Moreover, God is spirit, without any physical form. He is an invisible being without a body. The apostle John concurs: "No one has seen God at any time" (John 1:18). Jesus says, "Not that anyone has seen the Father" (John 6:46). Paul adds that God "alone possesses immortality and dwells in unapproachable light, whom no man has seen or can see" (1 Tim. 6:16). John states again, "No one has seen God at any time" (1 John 4:12).

The "face" of God represents the display of His glory. God does not have a literal face. Neither does He have arms, hands, feet, or body parts. When this language appears in Scripture, it uses anthropomorphic expressions in which infinite God communicates Himself to finite man in ways that we can understand. God is so far beyond our comprehension that He must speak to us in the most elementary terms. He must use metaphors to give us some understanding of what is beyond our grasp. To see the face of God means to know and experience who He is. If we knew more of His majesty, we would love and adore Him more.

Here are the gracious restrictions the Lord gave to Moses: "Then the LORD said, 'Behold, there is a place by Me, and you shall stand there on the rock'" (Ex. 33:21). He needed to retreat a distance away so as not to be too close to the bright shining light of God's glory. He is told to hide himself in the cleft of the rock. This will provide a needed buffer between himself and God.

The Lord continues, "And it will come about, while My glory is passing by, that I will put you in the cleft of the rock and cover you with My hand until I have passed by" (v. 22). The blinding glory of God will pass before Moses in an amazing display of holy radiance. The cleft of the rock will be like a shield for Moses. He will hide there so that he is not consumed. Further, God will place His hand over Moses as a covering. This will be a second buffer.

Then God says, "Then I will take My hand away and you shall see My back, but My face shall not be seen" (v. 23). Here is a third layer of protection for Moses. He will only see the back of

God. He cannot look directly into the face of God and live. Moses can only see a partial glory—or the divine afterglow. He cannot bear to behold the full revelation of who God is. Nevertheless, this protected view of divine glory is more than what he presently possesses.

A CLOSER ENCOUNTER

Each one of us needs a closer encounter with this awesome God. We, too, face similar pressures in life, much like those that confronted Moses. How will *you* endure the demanding trials of your life? How will you persevere in the face of many hardships? How will we each survive in a world that persecuted the prophets of God and crucified the Lord Jesus Christ? How will you remain steadfast amid countless stresses? The answer lies in what Moses dared to request—a deeper knowledge of God.

Do you want to know God's will for your life? The primary key to discerning the path God has chosen for you is to pursue the knowledge of His glory. Do you have decisions to make? Do you have mounting challenges you are facing? Then pray this earnest prayer: "God, show me Your glory!" No matter where we are in life's journey, none of us has reached the full knowledge of God. We all need to pray this heartfelt plea. As we behold more of His glory and majesty, we will see more clearly who we are and our direction in the plan of God.

Is your spiritual heart sluggish and lukewarm? There is one sure cure. Every one of us needs to pray with Moses, "Show me Your glory!" A growing knowledge of God enables us to live with enlarged faith in the midst of the storms of life. The only way we will be anchored firmly in the will of God and not be swayed by the turbulence of this world is by personally experiencing the far greater understanding of the character of God. A deepening knowledge of God's glory will ignite our hearts with a blazing love for Him—and trust in Him.

Do you desire to know more of who God is? Do you long to have a deeper relationship with Him? If so, pray this prayer that Moses cried out. Ask God to reveal more of Himself to you. This is a prayer that God delights to answer.

Chapter Two

INTENSELY PERSONAL

The Glory of God II

The ultimate end of all things that come to pass,
including the ultimate end of the great drama of redemption,
is found in the glory of the eternal God.

—J. GRESHAM MACHEN

Once we come to know God, we must seek to know Him more fully for who He is. Eternal life is personally knowing God and His Son, Jesus Christ (John 17:3). After the new birth, the Christian life is marked by a growing and deepening knowledge of God. Spiritual growth involves our experiencing closer fellowship with Him in a more intimate relationship. He will make His glory known to the one who humbles himself before Him and trembles at His word (Isa. 66:2).

This is precisely what God sees in Moses. He perceives a man who longs to know Him more closely. Moses has been given the most difficult assignment from God anyone could have received. He has been divinely commissioned to lead the nation of Israel out of Egyptian bondage into the promised land. But this divine charge is accompanied by many demanding challenges. He will have many seemingly insurmountable difficulties come across his path. Given these mounting obstacles, Moses desperately needs a greater knowledge of God and the strength He provides.

We want to continue our investigation of the dramatic scene in which Moses asks God to show him more of His glory. In the last chapter, we noted that God is self-revealing, autonomous, and awesome. We will now discover more aspects of what God is like.

GOD IS PERSONAL

The narrative continues, "Now the LORD said to Moses, 'Cut out for yourself two stone tablets like the former ones, and I will write on the tablets the words that were on the former tablets which you shattered'" (Ex. 34:1). The divine law given to Moses contains a clear revelation of the glory of God. The written statutes from God reveal His supreme authority and solemn right to command our lives. These Ten Commandments reveal His absolute holiness as He distinguishes between what is right and wrong. They also show His perfect righteousness as He promises blessings or curses dependent upon a person's response. The law is a good instrument, because it reveals the moral purity of Almighty God.

God directed Moses: "So be ready by morning, and come up in the morning to Mount Sinai, and present yourself there to Me on the top of the mountain. No man is to come up with you, nor let any man be seen anywhere on the mountain; even the flocks and the herds may not graze in front of that mountain" (vv. 2–3). Here, God adds another protective restriction. No other man is to come with Moses. This encounter will be too dangerous for anyone else to be there. This is because, as we have seen, no one can see God and live. This meeting is to be an individual experience intended exclusively for Moses. It is to be a one-on-one rendezvous with God that is to be intensely private and personal.

Moses did exactly as he had been instructed by God. "So he cut out two stone tablets like the former ones, and Moses rose up early in the morning and went up to Mount Sinai, as the LORD had commanded him, and he took two stone tablets in his hand" (v. 4). Without any delay, Moses immediately obeyed God. As he headed up the mountain, it was to fulfill a divine appointment with God. Moses requested this divine encounter, and he is about to experience God in ways that he never imagined. He is about to witness the glory of God to a degree he never knew before. Moses is undoubtedly filled with intense emotions as he anticipates this meeting with the Holy One.

Like Moses, we, too, need to individually meet with God. It can happen while we are alone with God in our Bible reading and prayer. It can happen while we are in the public worship of God. Or it can occur in a small group. Whatever the situation, we need to meet with God in His Word, prayer, worship, and meditation on His holy character.

A popular phrase during the Protestant Reformation was *coram Deo*, which means "before the face of God." Wherever we live, work, or attend church, we need to meet with God as though we are living where Moses finds himself—in the immediate presence of God. This divine pursuit needs to color every conversation, every form of entertainment, everything we read, every place we go, and everything we do.

GOD IS NEAR

Notice the spectacular way God draws near to Moses. "The Lord descended in the cloud and stood there with him as he called upon the name of the Lord" (Ex. 34:5). The cloud in which God descended is the same glory cloud that guided Moses and Israel out of Egypt (Ex. 13:21). It is the same cloud that guarded Moses and the Israelites at the Red Sea (Ex. 14:20). It is the same cloud that descended onto the mountain when God first gave the law (Ex. 19:16). This says God descended *in* the cloud, as though riding it like a conqueror in a golden chariot.

This cloud is yet another protective filter to prevent Moses from being overwhelmed by the glory of God. The divine light that came shining out of this cloud functioned as a restrictive screen. This is so Moses could not directly gaze upon the full manifestation of God in this blazing glory as He comes near.

But this dramatic encounter between God and Moses continues to intensify. God Himself actively begins to preach to Moses: "Then the Lord passed by in front of him and proclaimed, 'The Lord, the Lord God, compassionate and gracious, slow to anger, and abounding in lovingkindness and truth; who keeps lovingkindness for thousands, who forgives iniquity, transgression and sin; yet He will by no means leave the guilty unpunished, visiting the iniquity of fathers on the children and on the grandchildren to the third and fourth generations'" (Ex. 34:6–7). This sermon is an incredible self-disclosure by God. In this declaration, He reveals to Moses both His name and His nature.

GOD IS INDEPENDENT

First, God proclaims His name, saying, "The LORD, the LORD God." He repeats His personal name, Yahweh, giving it emphasis. *Yahweh* is from the same root word that God had earlier used in making Himself known to Moses at the burning bush, saying, "I AM WHO I AM" (Ex. 3:14). *Yahweh* is from the Hebrew word meaning "to be," meaning God is the self-existent One. This divine name reveals so much about Himself—that He is self-sufficient, eternal, without beginning, without end, unchanging, forever the same, never increasing, never decreasing, independent, and autonomous. It means God is dependent on no one for anything, yet everyone is dependent on Him for everything. God is the living, life-giving, all-sustaining One.

When God preaches His name, "the LORD," He is also declaring that He is the One who was, who is, and who shall be forever. This is the self-existence of God—or His aseity, which we will consider in greater detail in a future chapter. Here is the autonomous independence of God. He finds the grounds of His existence entirely in Himself. He *is* life, the living God, who gives life to all. There is no one propping Him up or sustaining Him. He is self-contained and self-sufficient, lacking in absolutely nothing.

The question is asked, Why did God create man? The answer is often proposed, "Because He was lonely." But the truth is, God was never lonely and has always been self-satisfied and self-sufficient. He has existed eternally as three persons in perfect fellowship—Father, Son, and Holy Spirit. Since before creation, They have mutually loved one another and have been perfectly satisfied with one another. They did not need anything else. They had each other.

The purpose of God in creating mankind was simply to showcase His own greatness for His own glory. The entire universe is simply a means for God to display His own grandeur. The psalmist proclaims, "The heavens are telling of the glory of God" (Ps. 19:1). The apostle Paul reaffirms the same, "For since the creation of the world His invisible attributes, His eternal power and divine nature, have been clearly seen, being understood through what has been made" (Rom. 1:20). All creation is for the glory of God—even you and me. We have a great need to know and glorify this God to fulfill our purpose for being.

GOD IS POWERFUL

The second name God uses in revealing Himself to Moses is "God" (Hebrew *El*). The Hebrew word *El* means "the strong one, the infinitely powerful one, the Almighty." If God is the Almighty, He has all might. He is the ultimate power in the universe. What little power we have is merely a delegated power, temporarily on loan from God. Sometimes people envision God and Satan in a tug-of-war between two equal superpowers. That is a grossly inaccurate picture, because God's very name is the Almighty (Rev. 4:8). As the strong One, He simply spoke, and everything came into being out of nothing. He has complete power over Satan and all the evil forces of this world.

Practically speaking, we should never question whether God can answer our comparatively small prayers. We should never wonder if He can provide us a job or living situation. We should never speculate if He can help our loved ones through their toughest times or give us the strength and encouragement we need in a crisis. Nothing is impossible for our Almighty God.

GOD IS SOVEREIGN

God further preaches His own divine nature to Moses. There is even more of God to be revealed than what He mentioned in His name. God preaches to Moses about His electing, redeeming, securing, sustaining, upholding, saving grace. In this powerful sermon, God proclaims that His sovereign grace is at the very heart of His glory. No one can preach like God—and no one can preach sovereign mercy like the One who chose and predestined His elect. No one can preach the sovereignty of God like the forever-reigning One.

When we get to heaven, the sovereignty of God will be far beyond our grandest thoughts of Him. God has given all authority in heaven and earth to His Son (Matt. 28:18). When Jesus returns, the Scripture depicts "many diadems" on His head (Rev. 19:12). These crowns represent sovereignty stacked on top of sovereignty. He has a name that "no one knows." This means no one can comprehend the full extent of His sovereignty. The unhindered exercise of His supreme authority is far beyond any human comprehension. At the heart of His kingship is the sovereign grace He exercises toward law-breaking, wrath-deserving, hell-bound sinners. What follows in this sermon by God is a manifold presentation of His reigning authority.

GOD IS COMPASSIONATE

God has already proclaimed to Moses His compassion—His graciousness or tender mercy: "I . . . will show compassion on whom

I will show compassion" (Ex. 33:19). He now declares a second time that He is "compassionate" (34:6). This refers to the tender affection He has toward those in distress, those who are suffering because of their sin. God is not a stoic sovereign, making impersonal chess moves in heaven regarding the lives of individuals. He is not a robotic ruler, devoid of any affections toward His people. In the depths of His being, God is full of fervent passion toward His chosen ones. This compassion is exercised by His sovereign will. When He said, "I . . . will show compassion on whom I will show compassion," He means it will be extended by His free and sovereign choice toward His elect. The basis will not be because of anything good in the one chosen, but solely because it pleased God.

God then preaches to Moses His *gracious* mercy. He announced that He is "gracious" (Hebrew *hannun*; v. 6), which means "to bend down or to stoop." This graciousness by God toward sinners is His condescending mercy that reaches down into the pit where we once lived in order to rescue us. Reaching down into the turmoil of this sin-plagued world, He lays hold of us in the refuse of this depraved culture to save us. By this gracious act, He freely bestows His mercy on the least deserving.

God next expounds His *patient* mercy. He announced to Moses that He is "slow to anger" (v. 6). This delay in exercising divine wrath is intended to give additional time for sinners to repent. He is slow to unleash His fury toward those under His wrath. Instead, God remains long-suffering toward objects of His holy vengeance. He is not in a hurry to inflict justice, but He gives sinners repeated opportunities for repentance.

This patience was clearly seen in the days of Noah. For 120 years, God kept a door of mercy open to this sinful world that was ripe for judgment. Patiently, God waited for more than a century for the human race to turn to Him in saving faith. The long-suffering of God is incomprehensible to mere mortals, who procrastinate in repenting and delay in coming to God in saving faith.

GOD IS LOVING

God further declares His *loving* mercy to Moses. He proclaimed that He is "abounding in lovingkindness" (v. 6). The English word "lovingkindness" is translated from the Hebrew word *hesed*. This is His loyal, steadfast love for His people. God's "lovingkindness" represents His unwavering faithfulness to love His own. Even when they wane in their love toward Him, they can be assured that "His lovingkindness is everlasting" (Ps. 136:1–26) toward them. This is to say, God is relentlessly unfailing in His love toward His chosen ones. He is unwavering in His devotion and unfaltering in His allegiance to them. When God saves a person, He permanently adopts him into His family forever. He says, "I will never desert you, nor will I ever forsake you" (Heb. 13:5). He always keeps this eternal covenant to love His own people.

Moreover, God pronounces His *reliable* mercy to Moses. He announced that He is marked by "truth" toward His children (Ex. 34:6). He does not misrepresent His devotion toward them. He does not pledge Himself to them one day, but then withdraw His love the next day. His "truth" (Hebrew *emet*) is firm, sure, reliable, certain, and dependable. Whatever God says concerning His loving devotion is unwavering. Isaiah says, "The grass withers, the flower fades, but the word of our God stands forever" (Isa. 40:8). What God says is forever true, even into eternity future. He will never alter what He says about His love toward His own. There is no editing of what He says in the Bible.

God likewise heralds His *boundless* mercy. To Moses, He claims to be the One "who keeps lovingkindness for thousands" (Ex. 34:7). "Thousands" could refer to a vast multitude of thousands of people. More likely, this mercy refers to thousands of generations to come. That being so, it means His lovingkindness will never be exhausted for endless generations to come. The mercies of God will extend to the end of time and far beyond, into eternity and without end.

God additionally expounds His *forgiving* mercy to Moses. In this sermon, God preaches that He is the One "who forgives iniquity, transgression and sin" (v. 7). He is a pardoning God, who wipes the slate clean of all sins by His abundant mercy. He makes this threefold repetition to forgive "iniquity, transgression and sin," which emphasizes not only the greatness of our sin, but the magnitude of His pardon. "To forgive" (Hebrew *nasa*) means "to lift up, carry away." God takes away our sins and places them on our innocent Substitute, Jesus Christ. Though our sins rise up to the heights of heaven, God delights in removing them from us by placing them on Christ at the cross.

GOD IS PUNISHING

God, as well, taught His *undeserved* mercy to Moses. With this bold statement, He explains, "Yet He will by no means leave the guilty unpunished" (v. 7). After His heavy emphasis on divine grace, God will not have Moses conclude that He views sin lightly. Those outside the circle of His love will be severely punished for their iniquities. They will be made the objects of His strictest justice and eternal punishment.

During the days of Noah, God drowned the entire human race with the exception of one family. He would have been justified to have done so for just one sin. How overwhelming must this wrath have been against the entire human race. It is this judgment on sin that makes His forgiveness so astonishing. God shows undeserved and unmerited mercy even to the chief of sinners.

Finally, God broadcasts His *protecting* mercy in this sermon to Moses. He says that He is "visiting the iniquity of fathers on the children and on the grandchildren to the third and fourth generations" (v. 7). This does not mean the future generations are declared guilty because of the sin of their fathers. But it does mean there are inevitable consequences to sin that are passed down from one generation to the next generation. There is an evil influence that is set in motion by one generation that infects the generations that follow. The point is that sin affects others for a long time. Paul writes, "Do not be deceived, God is not mocked; for whatever a man sows, this he will also reap" (Gal. 6:7). There is always a bitter harvest for future generations to reap from the seeds of sin being sown today.

GOD IS WORTHY

There is only one proper response to this divine manifestation of the glory of God—and that is worship. As a direct result of this sermon, the text says, "Moses made haste to bow low toward the earth and worship" (Ex. 34:8). Moses feels a sense of urgency to respond to this divinely proclaimed message. This sermon creates an immediacy in Moses to worship God. He feels compelled to act at once upon what he heard. There is a sense of the *now* as he has been under the preaching of God. Moses does not go home and pray about it. When God preaches, it is necessary to respond *right now.*

The knowledge of God always calls for an immediate response in the lives of those to whom He reveals Himself. Whenever God makes Himself known to us, we must respond with immediacy to worship Him.

"Moses made haste to bow low toward the earth and worship" (Ex. 34:8). He lowers himself in utter submission and total surrender to God. He responds in complete yieldedness to Him. He humbles himself beneath the mighty hand of God and worships Him. This servant of God could not stand upright in His presence—not after such a display of His sovereign mercy. He has to fall before God in humble reverence and acknowledge the worthiness that belongs to Him alone. In the New Testament, one of the words for worship (Greek *proskuneō*) means "to kiss toward." Worship is showing loving affection for God and is, in essence, like kissing toward God.

A greater vision of the glory of God, such as Moses received, leads to greater worship of Him. High theology from God ignites high doxology toward Him. The Word of God produces the worship of Him. This revelation about God produces our reverence for Him. There is only one thing that causes true worship, and that is for God to be known and adored for who He is—and for what He has done for us in Christ.

THE GREATEST PRIORITY

This must be the chief pursuit of our lives today. God must be the greatest priority in our life. We must seek to know more of His glory with everything in our being. Every decision we make must have God as our primary concern. Wherever will most magnify God must be our highest priority. We must not look for what is easiest in life. We must not choose the path of least resistance. Neither must we follow the crowd for fame and fortune. We must not pursue what looks the most appealing. Instead, we must prioritize the glory of God in all that we do.

Whatever will most honor God is the path we must choose. May every one of us pray what Moses prayed. May we seek to know God more fully, love Him more deeply, and behold His glory more closely. May God fulfill this request in our lives.

Chapter Three

MYSTERIOUSLY THREE

The Triunity of God

Nothing will so enlarge the intellect and magnify the whole soul of a man as a devout, earnest, continued investigation of the whole subject of the Trinity.

—C.H. Spurgeon

In our study of God, we must start with the most difficult aspect of His divine being to understand. The doctrine of the Trinity is the most mind-stretching truth when it comes to understanding who God is. This is the truth that there is one God who exists in three distinct persons—Father, Son, and Holy Spirit. Each of the three persons of the Godhead is God—the Father, the Son, and the Spirit are each fully God. Each of these three divine persons is coequal and coeternal with the other persons of the Trinity. As one God, the three persons share the exact same divine nature.

God is infinite in His being, and He far surpasses what our restricted minds can comprehend. The triunity of God is a subject so profound that it is a challenge to wrap our finite minds around it. While it is a truth that is far beyond our limited human capacity to understand, it is nevertheless necessary to believe in order to have a right understanding of who God is. Moreover, it is a truth necessary to affirm in order to hold to virtually every other Christian doctrine.

Granted, the word *Trinity* is not found in the Bible. But this fundamental truth is unmistakably taught in the pages of Scripture. *Trinity* comes from the Latin word *trinitas*, which means "threeness," referring to the triunity of God. Careful study of the Scripture is required to grasp the basic parts of this core doctrine about God. To deny the Trinity is to deny the deity of Jesus Christ. Consequently, to deny His deity is to deny the sufficiency of His atoning death to save sinners. This teaching is the cornerstone truth of the gospel. A denial of the Trinity robs the entire gospel of its saving power. The truth of His triunity is *that* important.

Because of the difficulty of understanding how there can one God in three persons, some people reject this truth. But it is irrational to only believe what we can fully understand. If that is the requirement to believe a truth in the Bible, we will reject virtually every major doctrine it teaches. For example, who can really understand how Jesus Christ is truly God *and* truly man? The answer is, none of us. Yet to reject this truth is to reject the gospel itself. Jesus must be truly God *and* truly man in order to die a sin-bearing, substitutionary death on the cross and take away the sins of His people. Or who among us can actually comprehend how the Bible is divinely inspired, *yet* also written by human authors? If it is the Word of God, then how is it that each biblical writer uses his own personality and vocabulary?

The answer is that none of us can fully apprehend these

profound yet fundamental truths. These doctrines must be received by faith in the God who has revealed them. With all that said, can we fully comprehend that one God exists in three persons? We cannot truly understand all that the Trinity means, but we must believe it by faith. In order to best understand the triunity of God, the following basic truths are essential.

GOD IS ONE

The most fundamental teaching of the Scripture is this cornerstone truth, that there is only one God. The first verse in the Bible declares this: "In the beginning God created the heavens and the earth" (Gen. 1:1). This one God spoke into being everything out of nothing.

Moses records in the great *Shema*: "Hear, O Israel! The LORD is our God, the LORD is one!" (Deut. 6:4). This simple statement of faith strongly declares a monotheistic view of God. The true God is the one and only God revealed in the Bible. He is not the so-called god of any other religion. Moses also states, "To you it was shown that you might know that the LORD, He is God; there is no other besides Him" (Deut. 4:35). Moses then reinforces this truth: "Know therefore today, and take it to your heart, that the LORD, He is God in heaven above and on the earth below; there is no other" (Deut. 4:39). Nothing could be more clear than this pronouncement that the God of the Bible is the one and only true God.

God Himself subsequently announces through His prophet Moses, "I am He, and there is no god besides Me; it is I who put to death and give life. I have wounded and it is I who heal, and there is no one who can deliver from My hand" (Deut. 32:39).

This divine declaration recorded by Moses affirms the singular existence of the one true God revealed in Scripture. Apart from Him, there is no other god.

When ancient Israel was confronted with their worship of false deities, God declares, "Before Me there was no God formed, and there will be none after Me" (Isa. 43:10). There can be no mistaking that God claims to be the only God. Again, God emphatically exclaims, "There is no God besides Me" (Isa. 44:6). God adamantly claims that He alone is God. He reinforces this again, "I am the LORD, and there is no other; besides Me there is no God. . . . There is no one besides Me. I am the LORD, and there is no other" (Isa. 45:5–6). Any other god is a counterfeit impostor, a false deity conjured up by the darkened minds of fallen men.

Jesus quotes the *Shema* when asked about the greatest commandment: "The Lord our God is one Lord" (Mark 12:29). This resolutely reaffirms what was taught earlier by the prophets. The apostle Paul concurs, "There is but one God, the Father, from whom are all things and we exist for Him" (1 Cor. 8:6). Later, Paul adds, "For there is one God, and one mediator also between God and men, the man Christ Jesus" (1 Tim. 2:5). James affirms: "You believe that God is one. You do well; the demons also believe, and shudder" (James 2:19). Even hell itself knows this truth. In any survey of Scripture, there can be no mistaking that there is only one God.

GOD IS THREE

At the same time, this one God exists in three persons in the Trinity. As stated earlier, the Bible teaches that the Father is God. Scripture also affirms that the Son is God, and it establishes that the Holy Spirit is God. All three persons are truly God, as much

God as the other two members of the Godhead. They are three divine persons who are coequal and coeternal. The three persons of the Trinity can be distinguished from the others in terms of Their personal properties, but not in terms of being or substance (personal properties refer to relations of origin otherwise known as *opera ad intra*).

Their personal properties mean that the Father is unbegotten, the Son is begotten of the Father, and the Spirit proceeds from the Father and the Son. Ancient heresies confused this truth and linger to this day. Nevertheless, the Bible teaches that the Father is distinct from the Son and the Spirit. The Son is not the Father or the Spirit. The Spirit is not the Father or the Son. Each person of the Trinity is His own person in the one Godhead.

Several passages of Scripture reference each person of the Godhead as distinct, yet They are one God. In the Great Commission, Jesus charges His disciples, "Go therefore and make disciples of all the nations, baptizing them in the name of the Father and the Son and the Holy Spirit" (Matt. 28:19). Here, Jesus commands His followers to make converts and baptize them in the name of the three persons of the Trinity. The word "and" distinguishes each divine person from the other. They are not one person, but three distinct persons. Likewise, Jesus did not use the plural verb "are," but used the singular "is." Neither did He say "names" in the plural, but said "name" singular—one God, one name.

Other important texts distinguish the three persons of the Godhead, such as in the baptism of Jesus Christ (Matt. 3:13–17). As God the Son went down into the water, God the Father spoke from heaven and God the Spirit descended upon Him. This three-fold distinction is also found in the final benediction of Paul's second epistle to the Corinthians. The apostle concludes this letter by saying, "The grace of the Lord Jesus Christ, and the love of God, and the fellowship of the Holy Spirit, be with you all" (2 Cor. 13:14). Here, all three persons of the Godhead are clearly distinct. Again, the word "and"—not "or"—distinguishes the three divine persons (cf. Rev. 1:4–5).

The Bible concludes with this distinction between the three different persons of the Trinity: "Grace to you and peace, from Him who is and who was and who is to come, and from the seven Spirits who are before His throne, and from Jesus Christ, the faithful witness, the firstborn of the dead, and the ruler of the kings of the earth" (Rev. 1:4–5). John would not have placed the Spirit between the Father and the Son if he had not regarded the Spirit as divine.

GOD IS ETERNAL

This one God, who exists as three persons, is also eternal. He is without beginning, eternally the same in His divine being. The universe is not eternal. Nor is any person eternal. Everything created has a point of beginning—but God does not. God is uncreated and therefore eternal. Further, each member of the Trinity is eternal, without beginning. All three persons in the Godhead—Father, Son, and Holy Spirit—are uncreated. We want to establish the eternality of each one of the divine persons.

To begin with, God the Father is eternal. Moses writes: "Lord, You have been our dwelling place in all generations. Before the mountains were born or You gave birth to the earth and the world, even from everlasting to everlasting, You are God" (Ps. 90:1–2). The psalmist extols God: "Your throne is established from of old; You are from everlasting" (Ps. 93:2). That is to say,

God—referring to God the Father—has perpetually governed the world from all eternity past. There was no start to the administration of His reign. The prophet Isaiah said God is the "One who lives forever, whose name is Holy" (Isa. 57:15). The prophet Habakkuk asks, "Are You not from everlasting, O LORD, my God, my Holy One?" (Hab. 1:12). This rhetorical question is, in reality, a statement, affirming God *is* "from everlasting."

The New Testament confirms this truth. The apostle Paul writes: "Now to the King eternal, immortal, invisible, the only God, be honor and glory forever and ever. Amen" (1 Tim. 1:17). Here, God the Father is described as "eternal," the One who has existed from eternity past. In addition, God the Father is the One "who is and who was and who is to come" (Rev. 1:4; cf. 1:8). This is to say, God the Father, who *is*, is God the Father, who *was*, throughout eternity past. Worded in a slightly different way, God is presently being praised as the One "who was and who is and who is to come" (Rev. 4:8). God the Father is God from eternity past, throughout time, and into eternity future.

Likewise, the Bible affirms that God the Son is eternal without beginning. The prophet Isaiah foretold the coming Messiah: "For a child will be born to us, a son will be given to us; and the government will rest on His shoulders; and His name will be called Wonderful Counselor, Mighty God, Eternal Father, Prince of Peace" (Isa. 9:6). This child to be born is "Eternal Father," meaning the One who eternally cares for His people like a father. The prophet Micah predicted: "But as for you, Bethlehem Ephrathah, too little to be among the clans of Judah, from you One will go forth for Me to be ruler in Israel. His goings forth are from long ago, from the days of eternity" (Mic. 5:2). This prophecy foretold that the coming Messiah would step out of eternity to enter time in Bethlehem.

The New Testament teaches the eternal preexistence of Jesus Christ. John records, "In the beginning was the Word, and the Word was with God, and the Word was God" (John 1:1). Jesus is the Word, who existed "in the beginning" (Gen. 1:1). When the heavens and the earth were brought into existence, Jesus—the uncreated Creator—was already in existence. Throughout eternity past, Jesus was "with God" (Greek *pros ton theon*). That is, He was face-to-face with the Father in closest personal fellowship. In His High Priestly Prayer, Jesus prayed, "Now, Father, glorify Me together with Yourself, with the glory which I had with You before the world was" (John 17:5). By this petition, Jesus acknowledges that He was with the Father before the creation of the world.

The Holy Spirit is likewise eternal God, without beginning. Being uncreated, the Spirit was present at the time of creation. In the second verse of the Bible, Moses records, "The earth was formless and void, and darkness was over the surface of the deep, and the Spirit of God was moving over the surface of the waters" (Gen. 1:2). This clearly testifies to the preexistence of the Spirit before the foundation of the world. The author of Hebrews writes, "How much more will the blood of Christ, who through the eternal Spirit offered Himself without blemish to God, cleanse your conscience from dead works to serve the living God?" (Heb. 9:14). Here, the Holy Spirit is described as "eternal," noting His existence in eternity past.

GOD IS EVERLASTING

This eternal God is also everlasting, meaning that He possesses immortality, life that is unending. Abraham called God "the

Everlasting God" (Gen. 21:33). The word translated "everlasting" (Hebrew *olam*) means "long duration, forever, evermore." Thus, God is incapable of dying or perishing. He will never know death or come to an end. Moses celebrated this truth when he sang, "The LORD shall reign forever and ever" (Ex. 15:18). This clearly teaches the perpetual existence of God. After God declared His name is "I AM WHO I AM" (Ex. 3:14), He exclaimed, "This is My name forever" (Ex. 3:15). In addition, God says, "I live forever" (Deut. 32:40).

Affirming this truth, Isaiah also calls Him "the Everlasting God" (Isa. 40:28). He will never cease to exist. David declares, "The LORD is King forever and ever" (Ps. 10:16). There will be no end to His existence and reign. Once again, David maintains, "The LORD sits as King forever" (Ps. 29:10). Moses writes, "From everlasting to everlasting, You are God" (Ps. 90:2). In other words, God is not only without beginning but without end. Jeremiah announced, "The LORD is the true God; He is the living God and the everlasting King" (Jer. 10:10). There will be no end to His reign as King over all.

The New Testament likewise states that God is everlasting. Paul asserts that He "alone possesses immortality. . . . To Him be honor and eternal dominion!" (1 Tim. 6:16). "Immortality" (Greek *athanasia*) means "undying." God will never die—He will never come to an end. He will never cease to be. He possesses dominion that is "eternal" (Greek *aiōnios*), or "that which is without end." Jesus Christ is also everlasting. The psalmist writes, "Your years will not come to an end" (Ps. 102:27). Again, the author of Hebrews maintains, "Jesus Christ is the same yesterday and today and forever" (Heb. 13:8). As already cited, John records that God "is to come" (Rev. 1:4, 8; 4:8). He is truly immortal as He gives everlasting life to His people forever.

GOD IS EXCLUSIVE

This eternal God is the only God. Beside Him, there is no other god. The first commandment states, "You shall have no other gods before Me" (Ex. 20:3). Any other so-called god is simply the result of the vain thoughts of darkened minds. Any other deity has no basis in reality whatsoever. God is so forthright about this that when Moses reissued the Ten Commandments, God says again, "You shall have no other gods before Me" (Deut. 5:7). God is emphatic that He alone is exclusively God.

The Lord says, "I am the LORD, and there is no other; besides Me there is no God. . . . There is no one besides Me. I am the LORD, and there is no other" (Isa. 45:5–6). God pronounces His own solitary existence as God with negative denial and positive assertion. Again, God Himself forcefully affirms, "I am the LORD, and there is none else" (v. 18). Further, He announces, "There is no other God besides Me, a righteous God and a Savior; there is none except Me. . . . For I am God, and there is no other" (vv. 21–22). Once more, God reaffirms this same truth: "I am God, and there is no other" (Isa. 46:9). God will not allow there to be any other deity in human minds except Him. He is insistent that He alone is God. Paul reaffirms this when he writes, "There is no such thing as an idol in the world, and that there is no God but one" (1 Cor. 8:4). The apostle refers to these idols dismissively as "so-called gods" (v. 5). This sarcastic reference mocks these gods as nonexistent and with no basis in reality. The exclusive God demands to be worshiped as the only God.

GOD IS INCOMPARABLE

This triune God, who eternally exists in three persons, cannot be compared with any man-fabricated god. There is none to whom He can be compared. When Moses stood before Pharaoh, he said, "There is no one like the LORD our God" (Ex. 8:10). In the face of the countless false deities of Egypt, God Himself said, "There is no one like Me in all the earth" (Ex. 9:14). The true God is entirely unique, beyond any comparison. After God parted the Red Sea, Moses led the celebration of the God who delivered them: "Who is like You among the gods, O LORD? Who is like You, majestic in holiness, awesome in praises, working wonders?" (Ex. 15:11). The only answer to these rhetorical questions is, unquestionably, there is no one like God.

As Moses pleaded with God in prayer, he reasons, "What god is there in heaven or on earth who can do such works and mighty acts as Yours?" (Deut. 3:24). Again, the anticipated answer is a negative. There is no deity conceived and crafted by man that compares with the one true God. In Moses' farewell sermon, he declares to the new generation that is poised and ready to enter the promised land, "There is none like the God of Jeshurun, who rides the heavens to your help, and through the skies in His majesty" (Deut. 33:26). The emphasis is strongly placed on the uniqueness of God. There is absolutely none with whom to compare Him.

In Hannah's prayer of thanksgiving, she states, "There is no one holy like the LORD. . . . Nor is there any rock like our God" (1 Sam. 2:2). There is no one with whom God can be compared. David acknowledges this same truth: "You are great, O Lord GOD; for there is none like You" (2 Sam. 7:22; cf. 1 Chron. 17:20).

No deity, no angelic being, or no person can compare with the unequaled greatness of God. David again offers praise to God: "There is no one like You among the gods, O Lord" (Ps. 86:8). The greatness of God's mighty works distinguishes Him as being incomparable with anyone or anything.

Through the prophet Isaiah, God announces, "I am God, and there is no one like Me" (Isa. 46:9). By this claim, God declares that He is matchless and inimitable, far surpassing any comparison with other false gods that are fashioned in the depraved minds of spiritually dead men. Jeremiah pronounces, "There is none like You, O LORD; You are great, and great is Your name in might. . . . For among all the wise men of the nations and in all their kingdoms, there is none like You" (Jer. 10:6–7). There is no one, not even among the wisest men on earth, with whom God can be compared. God is without peer and without equal, the only true God.

OUR EXCLUSIVE LOYALTY

This undivided God demands our exclusive loyalty to Him. He alone is God, and He alone must be our sole trust and confidence. God and God alone must be our hope in this life and the life to come. He only is worthy of our supreme affection and strongest allegiance. As the psalmist Asaph pronounces: "Whom have I in heaven but You? And besides You, I desire nothing on earth" (Ps. 73:25). God must be our one and only rock and refuge.

Exclusive devotion is what God requires of us. Jesus said: "No one can serve two masters; for either he will hate the one and love the other, or he will be devoted to one and despise the other. You cannot serve God and wealth" (Matt. 6:24). Serving God through His Son, Jesus Christ, is always an all-or-nothing proposition. We can never merely dabble in a commitment to Him. He categorically demands our exclusive fidelity. We must reject all other gods and give Him our wholehearted devotion. God alone is God, and He only *must* be our God.

May we say with the apostle Paul, "One thing I do: forgetting what lies behind and reaching forward to what lies ahead, I press on toward the goal for the prize of the upward call of God in Christ Jesus" (Phil. 3:13–14). May this be our one goal—the pursuit of knowing this triune God through Jesus Christ. May all else be secondary—may *He* be primary.

Chapter Four

INTERNALLY SUFFICIENT

The Aseity of God

*God is self-existent; He has the power of being
in and of Himself. He depends on nothing
and no one for His existence.*

—R.C. Sproul

It is never an easy endeavor to wrap our minds around the nature of God. His divine being so far exceeds us that it is impossible to plumb the depths of His essence—nor can we scale its heights. Never do we feel more of a sense of intimidation than when we come to the immense subject of the aseity of God, the attribute that most uniquely distinguishes Him as God. Here is the most basic, foundational lesson about God, yet it is one that has such exceeding profundity.

Contained in this one small, obscure word is the entire self-existence of God. *Aseity* comes from two Latin words—*a* meaning "from" and *se* meaning "self"—and means "from self, to have being or existence within oneself." It means that God exists in

Himself and possesses all that He needs within Himself. That is to say, He is the all-sufficient Sustainer of His own being. He lacks nothing within Himself and needs nothing outside Himself. Yet, everyone and everything is dependent upon Him.

Deeper than the greatest oceanic trench, and higher than the most expansive sky, is the knowledge of God's extraordinary self-existence. He is beyond all the processes of space and time and is therefore immovable and unchanging. Without His all-sustaining presence, all creation and the laws of science would crumble. The universe would collapse without His sovereign and powerful cohesion of all order, all life, and all matter. His self-existence guarantees the existence of all else.

The aseity of God marks Him as distinctly different from His creation. Because God has always been, His eternality guarantees His self-existence. Nothing God created possesses self-existence. No person created himself. No animal or plant brought itself into being. Nor can any created thing sustain itself. Everyone and everything is reliant upon God for its origin and ongoing existence. Only God exists without beginning and maintains Himself by His own self-sustaining power. He is the uncaused first cause, the uncreated Creator, the unmade Maker, the unsustained Sustainer. No one upholds God. Nothing sustains Him. He is independent of everyone and autonomous from everything. Yet, all that He has made is—at every moment—dependent on Him for everything.

In this chapter, we want to investigate the foundational attribute of God's aseity. Several important truths need to be specified in our consideration of this divine reality.

GOD IS SELF-EXISTENT

As already stated, the aseity of God begins with an understanding of His self-existence. He is life, He possesses life, and He is the Giver of life. In the first verse of the Bible, Moses records, "In the beginning God created the heavens and the earth" (Gen. 1:1). Before anything was created, God already existed. No external power brought Him into being. Before God created any life, He already possessed life in Himself. All that God spoke into being finds its origin in Him. Everything He made remains continually dependent on Him. Yet He Himself is not dependent on something outside of Himself—not for anything. By Himself, He sustains and maintains His own existence, as well as the entire universe.

This aspect of God's self-existence was dramatically revealed to Moses at the burning bush. There, Moses encountered God in a theophany, a direct appearance of God to man. Moses approached a bush that "was burning with fire, yet the bush was not consumed" (Ex. 3:2). Any other bush would be consumed by this fire. But this blazing bush was strangely maintaining its own existence, because the self-existent God was in the bush.

In this startling encounter, God revealed Himself to Moses with the name "I AM WHO I AM" (Ex. 3:14). This divine name (Hebrew *ehyeh*, "I am") comes from the Hebrew verb for "to be" (*hayah*), referring to God's own being. This name for God declared that He is the sole self-existent One. He is entirely dependent on Himself for His own being. As God, He alone sustains Himself, yet nothing upholds Him. Also contained in this divine name is the truth that God is unchanging in His being, never evolving nor devolving. He is not the One who once *was,* but no longer *is.* Neither will He *become* something that He presently *is not.* Rather, "I AM WHO I AM" means that He is neither increasing nor decreasing in His being. He is forever the same.

Moses elsewhere writes, "Before the mountains were born or You gave birth to the earth and the world, even from everlasting to everlasting, You are God" (Ps. 90:2). He declares that from eternity past to eternity future, God is God. There has never been a time when God was not wholly Himself as God. God was never less than who He is, never less than who He has always been. The psalmist writes, "Your throne is established from of old; You are from everlasting" (Ps. 93:2). With profundity and sublime simplicity, God has always been God—and will always be God.

God announces, "Before Me there was no God formed, and there will be none after Me" (Isa. 43:10). No one preceded God or produced Him. No false deity will follow Him. He existed long before any man-made idol was crafted. And He will exist long after all false deities have crumbled and perished.

If anything exists at all, then someone or something must have always existed. If there was ever absolutely nothing, then nothing could possibly be in existence now. Everything cannot come from nothing. But if there is anything now, that necessitates that someone has always preceded it. That Someone must have the power of being within Himself. That Someone can only be the living God.

God is the only necessary being. This means that He cannot *not* be. Whoever and whatever exists is dependent on God as the one necessary, preexistent Being. All creation is contingent on the existence of God. The entire universe is dependent on Him for its origin. Every creature relies on God for its continued operation.

All creation is in a state of flux. All that is created is always changing from what it was into what it is. God is the only source of life for all that is in a state of becoming. However, God is never becoming. He will always and eternally be Himself. This difference between "being" and "becoming" shows the colossal difference between God and us.

GOD IS SELF-SUFFICIENT

Because God is self-existent, He must be self-sufficient. As Paul preaches in Athens, he asserts that God is not "served by human hands, as though He needed anything" (Acts 17:25). Simply put, the apostle reasons that God needs nothing. There are no deficiencies in Him. He has no shortfalls. He possesses no scarcity. His creation cannot provide Him with anything that He finds missing in Himself. He lacks nothing, while possessing everything. He has no inadequacies, no incompleteness, no gaps, no voids to be filled.

God is self-complete, possessing perfect fullness within Himself. Paul reasons, "In Him we live and move and exist" (Acts 17:28). Accordingly, God lives and moves and has His own being in Himself. He needs no support system to uphold Him. He is not dependent on anyone or anything outside Himself.

God is missing no vital element, no critical part. The strongest person can give Him no power. The smartest intellect can provide Him with no knowledge. The richest tycoon can give Him no resources. He is entirely complete in Himself. God is not supplied anything by anyone as though He is inadequate or incomplete. He is self-contained, having within Himself whatever He needs.

Paul writes, "For who has known the mind of the Lord, or who became His counselor?" (Rom. 11:34). This rhetorical question demands the emphatic negative answer: No one has ever instructed God on any matter. No one has ever told Him anything He does not already know. He does not seek anyone's counsel. He has no need for anyone's advice. His divine wisdom is fully able to perfectly address every matter.

Paul then asks a second question: "Who has first given to Him that it might be paid back to him again?" (Rom. 11:35). Once again, the implied reply is an obvious negative. No one has ever put God in the position of being indebted to him. No one has ever loaned God anything that He needs to repay. God is not obligated to refund anything to anyone. Thus, God does not need to pay back anything. All creation is indebted to Him—and He is indebted to no one.

The self-sufficiency of God is succinctly stated in Paul's next statement: "For from Him and through Him and to Him are all things" (Rom. 11:36). This means that all things are *from* Him in eternity past. All things are *through* Him within time. All things are *to* Him into eternity future. Nothing finds its existence apart from God. All things are *from* His sovereign will, *through* His sovereign activity, and *to* His sovereign glory. Put another way, God is the Planner, Provider, and Purpose of everything. Nothing comes into being from itself. Nothing proceeds by itself. Nothing exists for itself. Everything exists from, through, and to this majestic God.

GOD IS SELF-EXALTING

All that this self-existent, self-sufficient God does, He does for His own glory. God has no higher purpose than the magnification of His own name. As discussed in the first two chapters, the intrinsic glory of God is the revelation of His own supreme being. His ascribed glory involves the supreme honor that belongs exclusively to Himself. All God's purposes have this highest goal. He self-exists to glorify Himself.

David explains that whatever God does, He does for the sake of His own name. He writes: "He restores my soul; He guides me in the paths of righteousness for His name's sake" (Ps. 23:3). In every matter, God always pursues His own glory. David acknowledges this chief aim of the glory of God when he writes, "For Your name's sake, O LORD, pardon my iniquity, for it is great" (Ps. 25:11). This man of God understands that His forgiveness magnifies the greatness of His own name. Great forgiveness from God reveals the greatness of the person of God. Again, the appeal that David makes is to the highest purpose of God—the glory of His own name. David appeals to God, "For Your name's sake You will lead me and guide me" (Ps. 31:3). This is an appeal that God gladly hears.

Asaph makes the same earnest appeal to God: "Help us, O God of our salvation, for the glory of Your name; and deliver us and forgive our sins for Your name's sake" (Ps. 79:9). This psalmist asks God to lead him in whatever way will most promote His name. This is because God seeks His own glory above all else.

God emphatically says, "For My own sake, for My own sake, I will act" (Isa. 48:11). God so strongly stresses the exaltation of Himself in His actions that He repeats this twice—"For My own sake, for My own sake." The prophet Jeremiah says the same: "Although our iniquities testify against us, O LORD, act for Your name's sake!" (Jer. 14:7). The appeal he makes to God is to act for His name's sake. The prophet understood that God is perpetually self-glorifying.

The apostle exclaims this same truth: "For from Him and through Him and to Him are all things" (Rom. 11:36). "From

Him" means God is the *Architect* of His eternal purpose that includes all that will come to pass. "Through Him" means God is the *Administrator* who brings it to pass within time. "To Him" means He is the *Aim* of all things, meaning He has designed all that comes to pass to be for His own glory. Simply put, God is His own highest purpose.

Paul points to this same truth of God's own self-glorification when he writes, "There is but one God, the Father, from whom are all things and we exist for Him" (1 Cor. 8:6). All God's eternal purposes are for His own glory: "Just as He chose us in Him before the foundation of the world, that we would be holy and blameless before Him. . . . to the praise of the glory of His grace, which He freely bestowed on us in the Beloved. . . . to the end that we who were the first to hope in Christ would be to the praise of His glory. . . . who is given as a pledge of our inheritance, with a view to the redemption of God's own possession, to the praise of His glory" (Eph. 1:4, 6, 12, 14). Each of Paul's doxologies aim at the praise of the glory of God as His greatest aim in all things.

One such sweeping doxology is: "Now to Him who is able to do far more abundantly beyond all that we ask or think, according to the power that works within us, to Him be the glory in the church and in Christ Jesus to all generations forever and ever. Amen" (Eph. 3:20–21). God is more than able to do all things to the glory of His Son, Jesus Christ.

GOD IS SELF-CONTENT

Being self-glorifying, God is, therefore, self-satisfied within Himself. He is fully content and exceedingly joyful with the exaltation of His own name. Paul writes that God is "the blessed and only

Sovereign" (1 Tim. 6:15). The word "blessed" (Greek *makarios*) can mean "happy, content, fulfilled." God is perfectly glad within Himself. No panic troubles Him. No lack of happiness depresses His own being. He is free from any inward frustration. No anxiety weighs Him down. He is deeply joyful with unending peace.

Nothing outside Himself controls His state of contentment. This truth reflects the impassivity of God, a truth we will consider in a later chapter. But for now, we agree with Jesus that everything the Father does is "well-pleasing" to Himself (Matt. 11:26). He enjoys perfect bliss as He moves history forward to its appointed end.

This inner happiness begins with the love that exists between the three persons of the Trinity. The Father loves the Son and the Holy Spirit, and He finds great pleasure in Them. The Son likewise loves the Father and the Spirit, resulting in His inexpressible delight. In a messianic psalm, David prophetically anticipates Jesus Christ saying to the Father: "Therefore my heart is glad and my glory rejoices; my flesh also will dwell securely. . . . You will make known to me the path of life; in Your presence is fullness of joy; in Your right hand there are pleasures forever" (Ps. 16:9, 11). A bond of perfect love unifies the Father, the Son, and the Spirit.

As "the only begotten God," Jesus Christ "is in the bosom of the Father" (John 1:18). This portrays someone reclining around a table for a meal and laying his head on the chest of the person closely seated next to him as they enjoy fellowship together. Being "in the bosom" represents the close relationship between the two people (see John 13:23). It is a position of intimate fellowship marked by sweet bliss. This mutual enjoyment is precisely how God the Son is represented in His eternal communion with God the Father. The converse is also true, as God the Father finds full-ness of joy with the Son and the Holy Spirit. Further, the Spirit finds pleasure with the Father and the Son. Here is the unending circle of the Trinity's mutual delight, as each member completely enjoys the others.

At Jesus' baptism, the Father announced, "This is My beloved Son, in whom I am well-pleased" (Matt. 3:17). "Beloved" (Greek *agapētos*) depicts the deep, abiding love between Them. This indicates the Father's perfect love for His Son. Likewise, the Son's obedience in His baptism, to fulfill all righteousness, demonstrates His love for the Father (Matt. 3:17). Paul further identifies Jesus as "the Beloved" (Eph. 1:6), meaning the One greatly loved by the Father.

God did not create the world because He had any dissatisfac-tion within Himself. There was no lack of happiness and joy in the Trinity. He had no unmet need. There was not an emptiness in Him that ached for fulfillment elsewhere. He did not need to create the universe because He was lonely. To the contrary, God was completely satisfied in Himself. The inner-Trinitarian rela-tionship between the Father, the Son, and the Spirit was marked by perfect bliss and joy. Further, God was well-pleased with all His works. Nothing He foreordained displeased Him. Nothing He has done brought Him any anguish. He delights in all that He predestined to occur. He knows that even the activity of evil is a forerunner to the good. Everything will conclude in subjection to Him—bringing Him ultimate glory.

GOD IS SELF-GIVING

Because God is self-sufficient, He is self-giving to His creation. He is the Provider of all life for all people in all places. John writes of Jesus, "In Him was life, and the life was the Light of men" (John 1:4). Therefore, all life is from Him, whether it be physical or spiritual life. As "the living God" (Rom. 9:26), Jesus says, "The Father has life in Himself" (John 5:26). As the Possessor of life, He is, therefore, the Giver of all life.

Again, Jesus claims, "I am the resurrection and the life" (John 11:25). This "I am" statement is a direct claim to eternal deity. Jesus is saying that He is coequal and coeternal with the One who spoke from the burning bush and said, "I AM WHO I AM" (Ex. 3:14). In the Upper Room, Jesus later repeats this same claim: "I am the way, and the truth, and the life" (John 14:6). This is to say, Jesus *is* the life, the One who alone *gives* life.

To the philosophically minded Athenians, Paul announces, "He Himself gives to all people life and breath and all things" (Acts 17:25). God gives life to all physical beings and, moreover, He sustains the life He gives. There is no life apart from God. It would be absurd to think that He, who sustains all life, should need to be sustained. It would be illogical to suppose that God, who supplies all needs, should need to be supplied with anything. God is not dependent, but independent, with all else dependent on Him. While everyone depends on Him, He does not depend on anyone. In God, all people live and have their existence, not vice versa.

OUR COMPLETE SUFFICIENCY

Because God is all-sufficient, we must look to Him to meet all our needs. He alone is our true source and sole supply. David writes, "The LORD is my shepherd, I shall not want" (Ps. 23:1). Left to ourselves, we sheep lack everything. We are totally helpless and defenseless, unable to care for ourselves. But under the Chief Shepherd's care, all our needs are abundantly met. We are constantly under the watch of Him who is inexhaustibly all-sufficient. As we look to Him, we will lack nothing that is good and necessary for enjoying life to the fullest.

Again, David states: "O fear the LORD, you His saints; for to those who fear Him there is no want. The young lions do lack and suffer hunger; but they who seek the LORD shall not be in want of any good thing" (Ps. 34:9–10). All our needs are met in our tender and limitless God.

The apostle Paul writes, "And my God will supply all your needs according to His riches in glory in Christ Jesus" (Phil. 4:19). When we trust our all-sufficient God, we will never lack whatever we truly need. We who believe upon Jesus Christ discover that "in Him you have been made complete" (Col. 2:10). We are made complete by Him who is all-complete, from eternity past to eternity future.

Chapter Five

UNIQUELY IMMORTAL

The Spirituality of God

The weightiest word in any language is its word for God.

—A. W. TOZER

F ew would challenge the fact that today, the church suffers from shallow and superficial views of God. The inevitable result of such trivial thoughts about Him is people who are tossed about like spiritual lightweights with little personal stability. Never has the need been greater to recover lofty thinking about the character of God. No generation of believers can rise any higher than its knowledge of the worthiness of God. A right understanding of His character is vital to Christian living. A high view of God leads to transcendent worship and holy living. A proper knowledge of God is likewise critical to the strength and success of any church.

How we perceive God defines how we view everything else. Our knowledge of God brings into sharp focus how we see the events around us. How we view Him shapes our view of politics and economics. It determines how we see the family unit and gender roles. It dictates how we view our vocational work. Our understanding of God becomes the prism through which we most accurately see our trials and adversities. It dictates how we view life, death, and eternity. The knowledge of God is the ultimate paradigm through which we rightly understand everything else around us.

To sharpen our focus about God, we must know Him as He truly is. Theology proper—the study of God—is the most important of all studies. Known as "the queen of the sciences," this endeavor examines the most profound subject in the universe—the Creator, namely, God Himself. Theology proper is that specified area of theology that addresses the being of God. It is critical to have a right understanding of the divine nature because it determines how we see every other area of theology. Moreover, it defines how we see ourselves. The proper knowledge of God is the accurate lens through which we see the world around us. Everything is shaped by our understanding of God.

In this chapter, we want to give attention to the spiritual nature of God's being.

GOD IS SPIRIT

A foundational tenet is that God is an incorporeal being without a physical body that can be touched or seen. Jesus says, "God is spirit" (John 4:24), which means He does not possess a corporeal form made up of a tangible substance. Jesus states, "A spirit does not have flesh and bones" (Luke 24:39). Therefore, God, who is spirit, is without material components. He does not have flesh and bones like what a human being possesses. He does not have a physical substance that can be touched or seen.

When Paul addressed the Athenians on Mars Hill, he reasons, "We ought not to think that the Divine Nature is like gold or silver or stone, an image formed by the art and thought of man" (Acts 17:29). By this statement, the apostle explains that God is unlike man-made idols crafted out of earthly material. God does not have a physical height that can be measured. Nor does He have natural substance that can be weighed on the scales. He has no concrete matter that can be grasped and touched. Being a spirit, He is without any bodily form.

Yet, verses that describe God as possessing humanlike body parts abound in Scripture. How do we understand these passages? Moses and the elders of Israel "saw the God of Israel; and under His feet there appeared to be a pavement of sapphire" (Ex. 24:10). The Scripture states that God "did not stretch out His hand against the nobles" (v. 11). Hanani says, "The eyes of the LORD move to and fro throughout the earth" (2 Chron. 16:9). Solomon states, "The eyes of the LORD are in every place, watching the evil and the good" (Prov. 15:3). Isaiah announces, "The mouth of the LORD has spoken" (Isa. 40:5). He also says, "The LORD's hand is not so short that it cannot save" (Isa. 59:1). God indicates, "My heart is turned over within Me" (Hos. 11:8). Paul writes about "the mind of the Lord" (Rom. 11:34). These verses ascribe to God human characteristics—eyes, hands, arms, brain, heart, mouth, and feet.

However, God does not have physical eyes with which He sees the world. He does not have an arm with a hand and fingers. God does not possess a brain that sends signals to His physical body. How do we resolve this seeming contradiction? The resolution is simple: these verses use the figure of speech known as *anthropomorphism*. This literary device conveys God in an easy-to-understand way as God makes Himself known with humanlike features. Through this device, we as finite creatures can understand what He is like. This infinite God must condescend to our level through such analogies to reveal Himself in ways in which we can comprehend Him.

When the Bible speaks of the eyes of the Lord, it vividly communicates that God is all-seeing. It stresses that God can peer into every person and accurately grasp every situation. The arm of the Lord simply means that God is almighty, the mind of the Lord reveals that He is all-wise, and the mouth of the Lord means He speaks with authority. But these metaphors require understanding this same reality—He is a spirit being without any body parts.

GOD IS INVISIBLE

Because God is an immaterial spirit, He is invisible to human eyes. Since He is without bodily form, He cannot be seen. The apostle John stated, "No one has seen God at any time" (John 1:18). Jesus says, "Not that anyone has seen the Father" (John 6:46). Paul identifies God as "the invisible God" (Col. 1:15). Again, he writes: "Now to the King eternal, immortal, invisible, the only God" (1 Tim. 1:17). Being "invisible," God is He who "dwells in unapproachable light, whom no man has seen or can see" (1 Tim. 6:16). The writer of Hebrews states that God is "unseen" (Heb. 11:27). Further, John writes, "No one has seen God at any time" (1 John 4:12). When someone looks for God, there is nothing for the naked eye to see.

This invisible God often chooses to reveal Himself as a bright, shining light. This beaming illumination is an emanation of the glory of God. When Moses petitioned God, "Show me Your glory!" (Ex. 33:18), God responded: "It will come about, while My glory is passing by, that I will put you in the cleft of the rock and cover you with My hand until I have passed by. Then I will take My hand away and you shall see My back, but My face shall not be seen" (Ex. 33:22–23). God revealed His glory to Moses as a blinding, effulgent light that could not be directly looked upon without resulting in death.

The only manifestation of God in human form is revealed in His Son, Jesus Christ. In the Upper Room, Philip said to Jesus, "Lord, show us the Father, and it is enough for us" (John 14:8). Jesus responded: "Have I been so long with you, and yet you have not come to know Me, Philip? He who has seen Me has seen the Father" (v. 9). In His response, Jesus claimed to possess the fullness of God's divine nature in a physical body. He is God made visible to human eyes. Jesus is called "the image of the invisible God" (Col. 1:15) and "the radiance of His glory" (Heb. 1:3). Extraordinarily, the incarnation of Christ made the invisible God visible.

GOD IS IMMANENT

Because God is without a physical body, He is immanent, meaning He is always near. We will examine this truth more carefully in a later chapter on the omnipresence of God. But for now, we understand that because God is a spirit without a body, He is everywhere present and thus is always near. He is always close at hand. No matter where we travel, the Lord is with us. He transcends all limitations of space, and He is present in every place with all that He is. Existing without spatial restrictions, God can be always near with His entire being.

Moses said to the nation of Israel, "For what great nation is there that has a god so near to it as is the LORD our God whenever we call on Him?" (Deut. 4:7). Ancient pagan gods were considered local or regional deities. But the one true God is always near, whether His people be in Egypt, the wilderness, or the promised land. David confesses, "Even though I walk through the valley of the shadow of death, I fear no evil, for You are with me; Your rod and Your staff, they comfort me" (Ps. 23:4). He declares, "The LORD is near to the brokenhearted" (Ps. 34:18). Elsewhere, the psalmist proclaimed, "The LORD is near to all who call upon Him, to all who call upon Him in truth" (Ps. 145:18).

The prophet Isaiah declared, "He who vindicates Me is near" (Isa. 50:8). That is, God is always present on the scene. Isaiah exhorts us, "Call upon Him while He is near" (Isa. 55:6). Jesus said, "Lo, I am with you always, even to the end of the age" (Matt. 28:20). No matter where we go, no matter what we encounter, no matter how alone we may feel, God is always with us in the great fullness of His divine being.

GOD IS PERSONAL

Although God is immaterial, He is, nevertheless, intensely personal. He is not an inanimate object or impersonal force. God is a personal being who knows, feels, and acts. He is not stoic. That is, He feels His affections to the maximum degree. He is fully alive, an infinite ocean of boundless being. He loves righteousness and hates unrighteousness. He hates sin and is angered by it. He rejoices in all that conforms to His own character. In addition, God decides and determines all that comes to pass. God is always identified with personal pronouns, such as *He*, but never as an *it*. All of this can be true of God only if He is personal.

Because this personal God is spirit, He is to be worshiped in spirit by people made in His image. Jesus said, "Those who worship Him must worship in spirit and truth" (John 4:24). He must be adored within the human spirit in response to the truth of who He is. Because God is invisible, we must come to Him by believing faith, not by detectable sight (Heb. 11:6). There must be no man-made representation of what God looks like to enhance worship. God said, "You shall not make for yourself an idol, or any likeness of what is in heaven above or on the earth beneath or in the water under the earth" (Ex. 20:4). There must be no graven image of God before the eyes of true worshipers. Any physical object that is purported to represent God, whether a painting or a statue, would be a grossly distorted and demeaning misrepresentation of the glory of who He is.

GOD IS INDIVISIBLE

Since God is spirit, without any component parts, He is therefore indivisible. He cannot be divided into segments in any way. This is known as the simplicity of God. There is not one part of God that is holy, while another part of God is love, and yet another part of God is wrath. He is not partly holy, partly loving, and partly wrathful. Rather, the entirety of His divine being is holy. The whole of His being is love. His whole nature is wrath. All these attributes are indivisibly intertwined as the whole of one divine nature.

Therefore, the love of God is a holy love. His truth is a holy truth, His wrath is a holy wrath, and so forth. Every attribute of

God is inseparably connected to the entirety of His being. Theologians sometimes call this God's simplicity, meaning He is not composed of segmented parts. Rather, God exists as one unified whole without any divisions in His being. There is not a part of God that is isolated from the rest of Him. Each of His attributes encompasses the whole of His divine being.

John writes, "God is Light, and in Him there is no darkness at all" (1 John 1:5). God cannot be cut up into parts like a layered wedding cake. There is not one part of God that is light, but another part that is dark. It is not as if His love is light, but His wrath is dark. Unlike the moon, God has no dark side. The entirety of God's being is radiant light without any darkness.

There is no aspect of God for which we need to apologize. Each attribute describes the whole of His being. To reject one attribute of God is to reject the totality of who He is. We cannot pick and choose which parts of God we accept and which aspects we reject. To refuse any one attribute of God is to refuse His whole being. This is because no single attribute can be separated from His whole person.

The indivisibility of God is also displayed in that there is no distinction between the divine persons when it comes to the divine attributes, because the three persons share the same being. No attribute is restricted to one member of the Godhead, but not found in the other two persons. Each attribute is equally complete in each divine person. Jesus is not more loving than the Father. The Spirit is not wiser than Jesus. The Father, Son, and Spirit are equally holy, equally omnipotent, equally loving, and coequal in each of Their divine attributes.

GOD IS UNITED

God is indivisible not only in His being, but also in His disposition toward creation, that is, in His sovereign will and eternal purpose. The three persons of the Trinity—Father, Son, and Spirit—are united in fulfilling Their mission. Jesus said, "I and the Father are one" (John 10:30), referring to Their shared purpose in redeeming sinners. Father, Son, and Spirit are perfectly one in aim and activity.

This indivisible union between the Trinity means that They are saving the same sinners according to the same eternal decree. Those whom the Father chose before time began (Eph. 1:4) are those whom He gave to the Son to be His bride (John 6:37, 39; 10:29; 17:2, 24). It is these same elect sinners for whom the Son came to redeem (John 10:11, 15). Further, it is these same chosen and redeemed sinners whom the Spirit is sent into this world to convict, call, and regenerate (John 3:8).

The Father will not choose one group of sinners while the Savior diverges and decides to die for an entirely different group of people. Neither is the Spirit calling yet another group to faith in Christ. Rather, the three persons of the Godhead act in perfect unity to save the same elect group. They are always working together, with the Father initiating, the Son accomplishing, and the Spirit applying the same salvation to the same individuals.

Consequently, we baptize "in the name of the Father and the Son and the Holy Spirit" (Matt. 28:19). This is because all three persons act as one in salvation. The three persons work together in the manner of a perfectly united team with one saving purpose to rescue the same individual sinners (Acts 13:48).

GOD IS INFINITE

As a spirit being, God is also infinite. This means He transcends all limitations of His creation, both within time and space. There are no finite boundaries that restrict Him. He possesses no constraints, except that He only acts consistently with His perfect being and will. He is free from any restriction that would be imposed upon Him by any people or circumstances. God cannot be contained by any temporal or spatial confinements. This eternal God is everywhere present with the whole of His being. Being infinite, He is not hindered by anyone or anything He has created.

The psalmist said, "Great is our Lord and abundant in strength; His understanding is infinite" (Ps. 147:5). The Hebrew phrase translated "infinite" (*ayin mispar*) conveys the idea that the full extent of His understanding cannot be limited. The vastness of His knowledge cannot be restricted or hindered. His power and intellect far exceed any imposed boundaries.

GOD IS INCOMPREHENSIBLE

Because God is infinite, He is incomprehensible to the human mind. Eliphaz rightly says that God "does great and unsearchable things, wonders without number" (Job 5:8–9). Job concurs that God "does great things, unfathomable, and wondrous works without number" (Job 9:10). Zophar challenges Job: "Can you discover the depths of God? Can you discover the limits of the Almighty?" (Job 11:7). These are rhetorical questions that imply a negative answer. No finite human mind can comprehend the incomprehensible God.

David declares that grasping the fullness of God is far beyond the ability of any man: "Great is the LORD, and highly to be praised, and His greatness is unsearchable" (Ps. 145:3). The greatness of God cannot be searched out. It far exceeds our capacity to comprehend it. Isaiah announces the same: "His understanding is inscrutable" (Isa. 40:28). We can know God relationally, but we cannot fully comprehend Him intellectually. An infinite God cannot be entirely grasped by His finite creatures. Paul states that the love of Christ "surpasses knowledge" (Eph. 3:19). The immensity of His grace cannot be traced by the human mind. It is too high for human understanding to scale its summit. God is too deep for man's thoughts to sound the depths of who He is and too high for us to fully ascend His heights. Though He reveals Himself to us, His incomprehensible nature means He cannot be known exhaustively.

Paul writes: "Oh, the depth of the riches both of the wisdom and knowledge of God! How unsearchable are His judgments and unfathomable His ways!" (Rom. 11:33). The magnitude of His greatness cannot be altogether discovered. Neither can it be completely known. The outer reaches of His grandeur are past finding out. Paul adds: "For who has known the mind of the Lord, or who became His counselor?" (v. 34). No one can instruct the infinite mind of God on any matter. Moses writes, "The secret things belong to the LORD our God, but the things revealed belong to us" (Deut. 29:29). God has chosen not to reveal all there is to know about Himself. The deep things of God belong to Him alone.

WONDER IN WORSHIP

These truths about God should propel our worship every time we come into His presence. Whenever we approach His throne of grace, there must always be a sense of awe, amazement, and astonishment to our devotion. We could never adore a God we could completely figure out. But because God is far beyond us, this realization should drive us to our knees. It should cause us to look up in wonder and amazement that the infinite One has made Himself known to us.

The reality of who God is far exceeds our comprehension. His divine character pushes us far beyond the limits of what we can understand. There are no limitations to His sovereignty or power. There are no restrictions to His knowledge and wisdom. There is nothing impossible for Him (Matt. 19:26). His ways are past our finding out. As high as the heavens are above the earth, so far are His thoughts beyond our thoughts (Isa. 55:9).

This is the God that we must come to know more deeply. Even though God is incomparable, we, nevertheless, must strive to know yet more of Him. No matter where we are in our walk with Him, there is still so much more of God to know. It will take all eternity to know God, yet even eternity will not be long enough to comprehend the infinite greatness and glory of our God.

Chapter Six

SUPREMELY REIGNING

The Sovereignty of God

Absolute sovereignty is what I love to ascribe to God.
God's sovereignty has ever appeared to me a great part of
His glory. It has often been my delight to approach God
and adore Him as a Sovereign God.

—Jonathan Edwards

The foundational truth of all Christian theology is the bedrock doctrine known as the sovereignty of God. It is the towering Mount Everest that rises above all that we confess to be true. The sovereignty of God is His undisputed right to govern all that He has created. This is His supreme authority—His absolute reign—over the entire created order. From God's lofty throne in the heavens, He actively presides over all the affairs of the universe. His universal government extends over all planets and peoples, over all events and outcomes. By the free exercise of His own will, God directs all the works of His hands with unrivaled majesty.

Every other doctrinal teaching must be brought into alignment with this cornerstone truth. The sovereignty of God means, quite simply, that God *is* God, not merely in name, but in the full reality of His kingship. That is, God always does *as* He pleases, *when* He pleases, *where* He pleases, *with whom* He pleases. No attribute of God recognizes His throne rights more than this truth.

Let us be clear: Good luck is not enthroned over the universe. Bad luck does not wear the sovereign's crown. Fortune does not hold the ruler's scepter in its right hand. The stars issue no royal decrees. Blind fate does not dwell in the heavenly palace. Random occurrences have no jurisdiction over the world. Chance happenings have no authority to dictate the affairs of men. Haphazard accidents have no basis in human events. Even human government cannot overrule the affairs of divine providence.

There is only One who occupies the celestial throne. This One wears the Sovereign's diadem and reigns from on high. He alone presides over all temporal affairs, over every life, and over each one's eternal destiny. The Lord God Himself—the Creator of heaven and earth—is this ruling King.

We want to trace out this titanic truth under several main headings. Each truth is an essential part of understanding the sovereignty of God.

GOD IS SUPREME

With unwavering clarity, the Bible declares the supremacy of God's reign over all that exists. David pronounces, "The Lord has established His throne in the heavens, and His sovereignty rules over all" (Ps. 103:19). The word translated "sovereignty" (Hebrew *malkut*) means "royal power, dominion, reign." This announces that God is above or superior to all others. He is chief, greatest, and highest, supreme in power, rank, and authority. Divine sovereignty means that God holds the position of the highest Ruler, reigning over all angelic and earthly powers. He is "the King of kings and Lord of lords" (1 Tim. 6:15). As the absolute Sovereign, God is governing every aspect of this terrestrial globe.

The psalmist announces: "The LORD reigns, He is clothed with majesty; the LORD has clothed and girded Himself with strength; indeed, the world is firmly established, it will not be moved" (Ps. 93:1). This bold declaration abruptly refutes any competing worldview that would presume that God *and* man co-reign together. It negates any notion that God *and* Satan jointly reign. It denies any religious superstitions that good or bad karma have any influence or sway. It rejects any pagan myth that random chance or fortune have any say. This announces that God—and God *alone*—rules over all.

This mighty chorus—"The LORD reigns"—is repeated four times (Ps. 93:1; 96:10; 97:1; 99:1). This anthem, written in the present tense, declares the strong testimony that God is presently exercising His will every moment of every day. He reigns in times of prosperity and disaster, in seasons of plenty and in famine, in life and in death. There are no boundaries on His jurisdictions. There is no statute of limitations on His reign. He was never put into office by the votes of creatures, and He will never be impeached.

Heaven and earth are run not by a democracy but by a theocracy, not by a majority vote but by the choice of One. The psalmist writes, "The LORD reigns, let the earth rejoice; let the many islands be glad" (Ps. 97:1). This should be the only rightful response to the announcement of the sovereignty of God—the rejoicing of the entire earth. Otherwise, we would have untold reasons to weep, because human history would be in total disarray and chaos.

Again, the psalmist testifies, "The LORD reigns, let the peoples tremble; He is enthroned above the cherubim, let the earth shake!" (Ps. 99:1). Because the Lord is enthroned in the heavens, all the peoples should tremble. They should be deeply sobered and be moved with fear toward such a Sovereign. This fact of His comprehensive reign should send awestruck reverberations through every human heart.

Once more, the psalmist announces, "But our God is in the heavens; He does whatever He pleases" (Ps. 115:3). With God enthroned on high, there is no successful resistance to the free exercise of His supreme authority. Even in the presence of many trials, His sovereignty remains unequaled, unrivaled, and unopposed. "Whatever the LORD pleases, He does, in heaven and in earth, in the seas and in all deeps" (Ps. 135:6). From the heights of heaven to the depths of the sea, God reigns as the Supreme One.

Nebuchadnezzar learned this lesson after being humbled to the earth—literally. After dwelling as a wild beast for a period of time, this powerful ruler exclaimed, "All the inhabitants of the earth are accounted as nothing, but He does according to His will in the host of heaven and among the inhabitants of earth; and no one can ward off His hand or say to Him, 'What have You done?'" (Dan. 4:35). His will cannot be thwarted. If God did not reign with omnipotence, He would not be God, but a mere lesser deity to be pitied. He is not idly watching the affairs of human lives, helpless, without any control over outcomes and destinies.

Instead, God is actively administering the affairs of providence every moment of every day. He is in complete charge of every person's life. Nothing lies outside the jurisdiction of His executive decrees.

During the turbulent hours of the first century, the apostle John had a vision of heaven and was permitted to peer into the unseen realm above: "Immediately I was in the Spirit; and behold, a throne was standing in heaven, and One sitting on the throne" (Rev. 4:2). As he gazed into heaven, what immediately captured John's attention was a "throne"—the throne of God. It "was standing," unshakable by earthly occurrences. This heavenly "throne" was a symbol of God's sovereign authority over the world scene. As the Sovereign One, He guides human history according to His charted course.

GOD IS PREDETERMINER

Before time began, God the Father was the sole architect of His eternal decree, which is His one master plan that encompasses everything that comes to pass. Paul writes that believers have been "predestined according to His purpose . . . all things after the counsel of His will" (Eph. 1:11). His "counsel" (Greek *boulē*) is His all-wise deliberation within Himself. From the beginning, God weighed every conceivable possibility for creation, history, and eternity. He could have created a thousand worlds as easily as the one He created. Drawing on His own perfect wisdom, He chose His "will" (Greek *thelēma*), the one divine decree for every event that comes to pass. This predetermined plan was so comprehensive that it included everything that would occur. Nothing lay outside this eternal purpose. It encompasses everything that will be.

Having chosen His eternal decree, God purposed to bring it to pass with unwavering resolve. This "purpose" (Greek *prothesis*) means "a setting forth." It describes the steadfast determination with which God executes His one plan (Rom. 8:28; 9:11). Nothing will prevent Him from the perfect execution of His will. God Himself guarantees that His sovereign decree will be executed by His fixed predestination. Before time began, the fulfillment of His eternal will was as certain as if it had already been fulfilled (2 Tim. 1:9).

The word "predestined" (Greek *proorizō*) means "to mark the horizon beforehand." It is a compound word, combining *pro*, meaning "before," with *horizō*, meaning "to mark the horizon." The idea behind *horizō*—from which we derive the English word *horizon*—was that the end of a traveler's journey was marked out on the distant horizon. In other words, the final destination was determined before the journey began. This makes the execution of the sovereign will of God irrevocable and certain, from before the world began (Rom. 8:29–30).

Included in the eternal plan of God is the salvation of His elect. In eternity past, the Father made a distinguishing choice of those whom He would save. Paul writes, "Just as He chose us in Him before the foundation of the world" (Eph. 1:4). The verb translated "chose" (Greek *eklegomai*) is in the middle voice, meaning God made this selection by Himself and for Himself. No one persuaded Him to make the choice He made. Nor did He look down the proverbial tunnel of time to observe what people would do and then make His choice accordingly. For reasons known only to Himself, God made His sovereign choice of many sinners out of the fallen human race.

Before time began, this choice was made by God the Father "according to the kind intention of His will" (Eph. 1:5). Here is an expression of the vast love of God—for you who believe in Christ. Paul records that those who believe do so because of "His choice of you" (1 Thess. 1:4). The apostle again writes, "But we should always give thanks to God for you, brethren beloved by the Lord, because God has chosen you from the beginning for salvation through sanctification by the Spirit and faith in the truth" (2 Thess. 2:13). By the mysterious exercise of His sovereignty, God "has chosen" His elect "from the beginning."

GOD IS CREATOR

As time began, God exercised His sovereign authority in the creation of the universe. In the free exercise of His will, God merely spoke, and everything came into existence out of nothing. The oceans did not create themselves. The stars and planets did not give birth to themselves. In six consecutive days, God made the created order precisely as it pleased Him. When God interrogates Job, He says, "Where were you when I laid the foundation of the earth?" (Job 38:4). God alone acted in His creativity and power—Job was to stand in awe of His completely sovereign wisdom.

The psalmist explains: "By the word of the LORD the heavens were made, and by the breath of His mouth all their host. He gathers the waters of the sea together as a heap; He lays up the deeps in storehouses. Let all the earth fear the LORD; let all the inhabitants of the world stand in awe of Him. For He spoke, and it was done; He commanded, and it stood fast" (Ps. 33:6–9). God effortlessly brought everything into existence by the mere breath of His mouth.

The psalmist reaffirms: "He established the earth upon its foundations. . . . O LORD, how many are Your works! In wisdom You have made them all; the earth is full of Your possessions" (Ps. 104:5, 24). Who could have resisted His will to create? The psalmist rejoices: "He commanded and they were created" (Ps. 148:5). Creation bears indisputable witness to the irresistibly sovereign will of God.

In the New Testament, we learn that God entrusted the act of creation to His Son, Jesus Christ: "For by Him all things were created, both in the heavens and on earth, visible and invisible, whether thrones or dominions or rulers or authorities—all things have been created through Him and for Him" (Col. 1:16). Everything that is was created by Him. The author of Hebrews concurs that "through whom [Jesus] also He made the world" (Heb. 1:2). This same author also states, "By faith we understand that the worlds were prepared by the word of God, so that what is seen was not made out of things which are visible" (Heb. 11:3). This act of creating by divine fiat was a vivid display of God's sovereignty.

GOD IS EXECUTOR

After creating the world, God began executing His prewritten decree for human history. Every event occurs according to His eternal script. God Himself declares, "I am God, and there is no one like Me, declaring the end from the beginning, . . . 'My purpose will be established, and I will accomplish all My good pleasure'; . . . Truly I have spoken; truly I will bring it to pass. I have planned it, surely I will do it" (Isa. 46:9–11). God speaks at the beginning, and He declares all that will occur throughout time.

From the dawn of civilization, God is director over the many events on the world stage. In the garden, God was presiding over the original sin of Adam and the fall of mankind into depravity. Though He is not the author of sin, this first rebellion was nevertheless a part of His divine plan. By no means did it catch God off guard. He ruled over the subsequent populating of the earth, the worldwide flood, and the dispersing of the nations from the Tower of Babel.

By His own plan, God called Abram out of paganism and created the nation of Israel. He reigned over the Egyptian bondage of His chosen people and their subsequent exodus. He led the Jewish nation during its wilderness wanderings and ushered them into the promised land, where He established the nation's theocracy. God oversaw the exile of the nation into the Assyrian and Babylonian captivities and brought them back to the land.

With supreme authority, God sent His Son, Jesus Christ, into this world to be born of a virgin, under the law (Luke 1:35; Gal. 4:4). God delivered Him over to death on the cross to bear the sins of His people (Rom. 4:25; 8:32). He commissioned the apostles and directed the spread of His kingdom through the fires of persecution. To this present hour, God is governing over all the affairs of providence. Moment by moment, He is causing all things to work together for the good of His people (Rom. 8:28).

God has not abdicated His throne. He is not on sabbatical. He is not a mere passive observer of world movements. To the contrary, God is reigning every moment of every day over the flow of human history—through every catastrophe to the greatest triumph.

GOD IS METICULOUS

God controls not only the big picture of world events, but also its most minute details. He orchestrates not only the macro, but the micro. God determines the day of everyone's birth and sets the number of their days until their death. Job says, "Since his days are determined, the number of his months is with You; and his limits You have set so that he cannot pass" (Job 14:5). No one will live one hour, minute, or second beyond the time God has appointed for them.

David writes, "Your eyes have seen my unformed substance; and in Your book were all written the days that were ordained for me, when as yet there was not one of them" (Ps. 139:16). David understands that all his days are sovereignly foreordained for him, long before he came into the world. The span of his life was predetermined by God and recorded in His divine book with indelible ink. The precise length of his life was decided by God before he was born—and nothing can thwart what He has decreed.

This overarching control by God is settled and sure, down to the smallest details in life. Even the most seemingly minuscule occurrences are under His overruling control. Solomon recognizes the control of God over a man's steps: "The mind of man plans his way, but the LORD directs his steps" (Prov. 16:9). Each individual step is fulfilling the eternal purpose of God. Solomon adds, "The lot is cast into the lap, but its every decision is from the LORD" (v. 33). Such a seemingly tiny event as the careless casting of a lot, used in ancient decision making, is guided by the invisible hand of God.

Though man plans his way, the purpose of God remains fixed and will be fulfilled. Solomon verifies, "Many plans are in a man's heart, but the counsel of the LORD will stand" (Prov. 19:21). Once more, Solomon confirms, "The horse is prepared for the day of battle, but victory belongs to the LORD" (Prov. 21:31). Though man must make his preparation, the outcome inevitably belongs to God.

Jesus says: "Are not two sparrows sold for a cent? And yet not one of them will fall to the ground apart from your Father. But the very hairs of your head are all numbered" (Matt. 10:29–30). The Lord asserts that even the smallest hair particles are under the control of God. The smallest occurrences in a person's life are but small threads woven by God into the larger tapestry of His predetermined plan. Paul writes, "And we know that God causes all things to work together for good to those who love God, to those who are called according to His purpose" (Rom. 8:28). Nothing lies outside the control of God for the good of His people.

GOD IS OVERRULING

No matter what resistance is mounted against God, He is determined to execute His sovereign will. Regardless of how Satan or sinners may oppose God, He cannot be moved from accomplishing His original decree. Man plans his way, but God overrules and causes His sovereign will to be accomplished. He will never deviate from what He purposes to do. He will never shift to a plan B. His will is inflexibly fixed. God is determined with immutable resolution to bring His eternal plan to completion.

Nothing can thwart the sovereign will of God. The psalmist declares: "The LORD nullifies the counsel of the nations; He frustrates the plans of the peoples. The counsel of the LORD stands forever, the plans of His heart from generation to generation" (Ps. 33:10–11). Though all the nations plot and take counsel against Him, the plans of the Lord cannot be altered. Even the most powerful rulers on the earth, working together in a global conspiracy against God, could not divert His purposes from advancing to their appointed end.

Solomon teaches, "The king's heart is like channels of water in the hand of the LORD; He turns it wherever He wishes" (Prov. 21:1). Even the most powerful rulers do His bidding. The prophet Isaiah boldly asks: "For the LORD of hosts has planned, and who can frustrate it? And as for His stretched-out hand, who can turn it back?" (Isa. 14:27). The omnipotent hand of God cannot be held back. He raises up one ruler and lowers another. God puts evil rulers in place to carry out His purposes. God is "the blessed and only Sovereign, the King of kings and Lord of lords" (1 Tim. 6:15), who rules the rulers of the earth to fulfill His own plan.

To be sure, Satan is not a power equal to God. The forces of darkness are not in a position to conquer God—not in the least. John writes, "Greater is He who is in you than he who is in the world" (1 John 4:4). The ultimate authority belongs exclusively to God. While Satan is real and more powerful than we are, he is nothing compared to God. There are some people who tremble at the thought of the devil, as though he is sovereign. But there is only one Sovereign—God Himself, and none can overcome Him.

Between the two appearings of Christ, Jesus is building His church, "and the gates of Hades will not overpower it" (Matt. 16:18). No matter how dark the world scene may become, nothing will prevent Jesus from successfully executing His worldwide mission of building His church. No matter how unbelieving the professing church becomes, Jesus will build and establish His *true* church. His overruling sovereignty guarantees its success.

The unbelief of the Jewish nation in the first century could not hinder the birth and growth of the church. On the day of

Pentecost, Peter proclaimed the gospel and confidently announced that "as many as the Lord our God will call to Himself" would be saved (Acts 2:39). In response to his gospel proclamation, three thousand people were called and converted by the sovereign grace of God. In the face of Jewish unbelief, Paul turned to preaching to the Gentiles, assured that "as many as had been appointed to eternal life believed" (Acts 13:48). Nothing can defy God's power or thwart Him as He builds His church—He is victorious over all.

GOD IS COMPLETING

Unto the completion of time, God will direct human history to its appointed end. In eternity past, He foreordained how the end of the age would transpire. In the future, He will direct all the nations of the world to find their place in this climactic consummation. He is Lord over the final acts of human history, because He has already predetermined it. Whether directly or indirectly, whether by direct intervention or by secondary causalities, God is bringing all things to their appointed end in fulfillment of His predetermined plan.

As the end of the age draws near, God has foreordained the rise and fall of every reigning monarch and world power. He has appointed the nations for their hour in history. He will put world leaders in their place—and so it will be. The apostle John was given a preview of the final world rulers: "For God has put it in their hearts to execute His purpose" (Rev. 17:17). God has prewritten the final scene of world history, and unbelieving kings and their pagan kingdoms will play their divinely assigned roles. By His sovereign hand, God will unilaterally bring human history to its consummation.

God has already foreordained the hour when Jesus Christ will return to this earth. On that glorious day, the elect will be gathered to Himself. Unbelievers will be judged. Satan will be cast into the lake of fire. The kingdom of God will be established. The new Jerusalem will be populated. The new heaven and new earth will be glorious. The saints will see God. They will reign with Christ. Every divine promise will be kept. Every prophecy will be fulfilled. Every divine purpose will triumph. Every enemy will be defeated. Every saint will be rewarded. This remarkable future rests in the hands of our trustworthy and sovereign God.

GOD IS ULTIMATE

In the end, the Father will lay all things at the feet of Christ. Jesus will then reciprocate and present it all back to the Father. Paul explains: "For He has put all things in subjection under His feet. But when He says, 'All things are put in subjection,' it is evident that He is excepted who put all things in subjection to Him. When all things are subjected to Him, then the Son Himself also will be subjected to the One who subjected all things to Him, so that God may be all in all" (1 Cor. 15:27–28). In the end, all things will be subjected to God the Father.

There will be no end to the eternal reign of God. Throughout endless ages to come, He will sit on His throne and perpetuate the free exercise of His supreme authority. God will reign as sovereign—"forever and ever" (Rev. 11:15). "Hallelujah! For the Lord our God, the Almighty, reigns" (Rev. 19:6).

OUR COMFORT IN CRISIS

The sovereignty of God is like a soft pillow upon which the believer lays his head at night. There is no attribute more comforting to God's children than the sovereignty of their Father. Under our most adverse circumstances, we believe that sovereignty has ordained our afflictions. In the most severe trials, we trust that God has a purpose, and behind that purpose is His master plan. Even in our darkest valleys, we must rely on this foundational truth, that divine sovereignty is using it as a part of a far greater design for His glory and our good.

In the lowest ebb of life, we may remain confident that God will use these difficulties to sanctify us. We are convinced that nothing lies outside of God's control. All things are moving forward by the inscrutable mystery of His eternal will. His supreme authority remains operative. His timing is perfect. His hand remains on us for good (Gen. 50:20).

All things—both good and bad, both prosperity and adversity—are being directed by God for a far greater good. If it was not for the sovereignty of God, we would despair. But because He remains on His throne, ruling over every storm of life, we remain full of hope, knowing it is all under His guidance.

Chapter Seven

INFINITELY HOLY

The Holiness of God

Holiness is the most sparkling jewel
of His crown.

—Thomas Watson

O ne singular attribute of God is the most supremely praised in heaven. This electrifying aspect of His divine nature is recognized above all other attributes by those who are in His immediate presence. The angelic beings—the seraphim—around God's throne are crying out day and night this one awestruck chorus: "Holy, Holy, Holy, is the Lord of hosts, the whole earth is full of His glory" (Isa. 6:3). Likewise, the four living creatures before the throne are proclaiming this same majestic anthem: "Holy, Holy, Holy is the Lord God, the Almighty, who was and who is and who is to come" (Rev. 4:8). This divine perfection—the absolute holiness of God—is always being announced in heaven.

The angelic beings before the throne are not shouting, "Love, love, love," although "God is love" (1 John 4:8). The heavenly host is not declaring, "Truth, truth, truth," although God is truth (Ps. 31:5). Rather, the angels are calling out, "Holy, Holy, Holy." They make this emphasis on the holiness of God three times in rapid succession—to elevate this attribute to the superlative degree. In other words, God is not merely holy as others would be holy. He is not simply holier than any of His creatures. Instead, this three-fold anthem proclaims that God is the single holiest being in the entire universe.

Everything about God is absolutely holy, and this one attribute uniquely defines His other attributes. His love is holy love, His justice is holy justice, and His mercy is holy mercy. Holiness gives shape to every other divine attribute. Everything about God is marked by His absolute holiness. This one characteristic is the sum and substance of His entire being. In reality, holiness is wholly comprehensive of all that God is.

God's name is "holy" (Ps. 145:21). Jesus addressed God as "Holy Father" (John 17:11). Likewise, Jesus Christ Himself is as equally holy as the Father. He was born the "holy Child" (Luke 1:35) and recognized by the demons as "the Holy One of God" (Mark 1:24). Peter likewise called Him "the Holy One of God" (John 6:69). In turn, Jesus called the Spirit of God "the Holy Spirit" (Matt. 28:19). In the Bible, the Spirit is called the "Holy Spirit" nearly one hundred times.

Moreover, the angels are described as His "holy ones" (Deut. 33:2). The Word of God is contained in the "holy Scriptures" (Rom. 1:2). The people of God are called "holy people" (Deut. 7:6). The temple in Jerusalem is the "holy temple" (Ps. 11:4). God dwells in heaven on His "holy mountain" (Ps. 2:6). The city of Jerusalem is "the holy city" (Neh. 11:1). The Sabbath is the "holy" day (Ex. 20:8, 11). The promised land is His "holy land" (Ps. 78:54). Holiness is the cornerstone of all of God's redemptive purposes.

As we survey the holiness of God, we will consider it under several headings.

GOD IS SET APART

The first use of *holy* in the Bible is spoken by God to Moses: "Do not come near here; remove your sandals from your feet, for the place on which you are standing is holy ground" (Ex. 3:5). This means the ground where God is manifesting Himself to Moses is set apart from the ordinary for this special purpose. In the Old Testament, the Hebrew word for "holy" (*qadosh*) means "separation." The idea behind this ancient word is the cutting of an object into two pieces. The holiness of God means that He is separated from His creation. He is completely set apart from everything He has made. In modern times, we would say He is "a cut apart." Put another way, God is "wholly other" than His creatures.

Because God is holy, He is distinguished from everyone and everything else He has made. Everything about God sets Him apart from man. An infinite chasm separates this holy God from sinful humanity. Moreover, God is entirely unlike any other god. Moses said to Pharaoh, "There is no one like the LORD our God" (Ex. 8:10; cf. 9:14). God is altogether set apart from His creation, in a separate category unto Himself. Moses sang, "Who is like You among the gods, O LORD? Who is like You, majestic in holiness?" (Ex. 15:11). The answer is categorically no one. No one else is even close to His characteristics. No one is in His class.

GOD IS TRANSCENDENT

The holiness of God also conveys His exalted transcendence. Being holy, God is exalted *above* His creation. The word *transcendence* means exceeding the usual limits, rising above the norm, surpassing an established limit. As applied to God, He exceeds His creation—He is far above and beyond His creation. Isaiah saw in his vision of God that He is "lofty and exalted" (Isa. 6:1). The word "lofty" (Hebrew *rum*) means "to be high, raised, uplifted, set on high," and "exalted" (Hebrew *nasa*) means "to be lifted up." The prophet beheld God in His holiness—exalted in the heavens, high above His creatures. He saw the transcendence of God over the world, far exceeding normal constraints.

David pronounces the same transcendence of God in His holiness: "You are holy, O You who are enthroned upon the praises of Israel" (Ps. 22:3). This declaration of His absolute holiness recognizes His lofty enthronement on high. Here, divine holiness and His exalted transcendence are inseparably connected. As the Holy One, He towers over His people. Thus, His holiness includes His sovereignty. He is elevated far above the works of His hands—ruling in might and majesty.

The enthronement psalms, which are Psalms 93–99, connect the holiness of God with His lofty transcendence. The psalmist announces: "The LORD reigns, let the peoples tremble; He is enthroned above the cherubim, let the earth shake! The LORD is great in Zion, and He is exalted above all the peoples. Let them praise Your great and awesome name; holy is He" (Ps. 99:1–3). This highly charged pronouncement declares holy God to be enthroned *above* all the peoples. The psalmist again lifts up his voice, "Exalt the LORD our God and worship at His holy hill, for holy is the LORD our God" (v. 9). God is enthroned on His holy mountain above those who worship Him.

GOD IS MAJESTIC

The holiness of God likewise includes another key component— His kingly majesty. Because God is holy, He is robed in regal splendor and dazzling in glory. In Moses' song, he rejoiced that God is "majestic in holiness" (Ex. 15:11). The word translated "majestic" (Hebrew *adar*) means "glorious, noble, great." It communicates the royal superiority of His stately kingship. David declares: "O LORD, our Lord, how majestic is Your name in all the earth, who have displayed Your splendor above the heavens!" (Ps. 8:1). He exclaims that resplendent grandeur adorns God in His magnificent holiness.

The psalmist further associates the holiness of God with His august nobility: "The LORD reigns, He is clothed with majesty; the LORD has clothed and girded Himself with strength; indeed, the world is firmly established, it will not be moved. . . . Holiness befits Your house, O LORD, forevermore" (Ps. 93:1, 5). Here, God, whose dwelling place is holy, is portrayed as wearing kingly robes of majesty. The psalmist again declares, "Worship the LORD in holy attire; tremble before Him, all the earth. Say among the nations, 'The LORD reigns; indeed, the world is firmly established, it will not be moved; He will judge the peoples with equity" (Ps. 96:9–10). Once more, the holiness of God is linked to His kingly reign and majesty.

This is exactly what Isaiah beheld in his vision of the holiness of God. The prophet observed God as "lofty" and "the train of His robe filling the temple" (Isa. 6:1). In ancient times, the greatness of kings was revealed by the length of their robes. The greater the king, the longer was his robe. In this revelation of God's holiness, His robe filled the entire throne room in the heavenly palace. There was no room left for the train of any other ruler. Not even the hem of another garment could be in the presence of heaven's King. This holy God is the only Sovereign.

To capture a vision of God in His stately holiness is always stunning. To behold Him in His majesty is breathtaking. God is spectacular in the beauty of His holiness. It is astonishing for us to contemplate the perfections of His regal character. When we gaze upon God in His holiness, we are overwhelmed. This exalted greatness of the Holy One is nothing less than magnificent.

GOD IS AWESOME

The holiness of God makes Him stunningly awesome to those who behold Him. Moses described God as "awesome" (Deut. 7:21). He said, "For the LORD your God is the God of gods and the Lord of lords, the great, the mighty, and the awesome God" (Deut. 10:17). The word "awesome" (Hebrew *yare*) means "to fear, revere, be afraid." The holiness of God instills the sobering reverence due His name. His holiness creates great respect for Him from those who encounter Him. The holiness of God causes men to be afraid of Him and even to be filled with dread. Because He is so wondrous, those in His immediate presence are overwhelmed and struck with awe.

This is exactly what Isaiah experienced when he was confronted with God who is "Holy, Holy, Holy" (Isa. 6:3). He was shaken to the core of his being. Even "the thresholds trembled" when God's holiness was declared (v. 4). Likewise, "the temple was filling with smoke." Even heaven itself is struck with a healthy fear of this awesome God. There is nothing casual about being in the presence of the Holy One.

Isaiah responded, "Woe is me, for I am ruined!" (v. 5). He was staggered to be in such close proximity to the holiness of God. "Woe" (Hebrew *oy*) is a passionate cry of deep grief or despair. In a word, he was devastated. "Ruined" (Hebrew *damah*) means "to cease, to be undone, to be destroyed." The prophet is fearful that he will cease to live because he is so near to this spellbinding God. He is shattered and even undone. Fearful reverence has gripped the trembling heart of Isaiah.

In like manner, Nehemiah addressed God as "the great and awesome God" (Neh. 1:5). These two descriptors—"great and awesome"—are used almost interchangeably. Later, he said that the Lord "is great and awesome" (Neh. 4:14), and once more, Nehemiah identified God in prayer as "the awesome God" (Neh. 9:32). Daniel addressed God in the same way as "the great and awesome God" (Dan. 9:4). The awesomeness of God is an indivisible part of His holiness.

GOD IS FLAWLESS

Another critical aspect of God's holiness is His moral perfection. He is perfectly sinless, possessing no blemishes in His character. Being faultless, God is completely pure in His thoughts, words, and decisions. God is marked by moral excellency in His being, nature, and motives. He is without any taint of sin in His thoughts and actions. He is unspotted and unstained in the entirety of His holy being.

The prophet says, "Your eyes are too pure to approve evil, and You can not look on wickedness with favor" (Hab. 1:13). The eyes of God are "pure" (Hebrew *tahor*), meaning "clean." He cannot look at evil with any approval. Holy God can never be indifferent to the sin He sees in His creatures. All sins, whether large or small, are vile and heinous in His sight. He cannot be morally neutral toward the sinfulness of His creatures. The point of emphasis here, though, is the absolute purity of God's eyes. He sees His creation with sinless vision.

Divine holiness means God is morally perfect. He is intrinsically spotless and pure. Jesus said, "Therefore you are to be perfect, as your heavenly Father is perfect" (Matt. 5:48). This means that God is entirely flawless in His character and choices. The standard by which He will judge mankind is His own moral perfection. He Himself is the unblemished standard that is set forth in "the perfect law" (James 1:25). Being inwardly untainted, God can never make a mistake. His word is faultless without any mistakes. His actions are always perfect and cannot be improved. His judgments are always right. He never renders a wrong verdict. Everything about God is infinitely and exceedingly pure.

GOD IS UNAPPROACHABLE

Because God is absolutely holy, He is, therefore, unapproachable by unredeemed, sinful humanity. David announces: "The LORD is in His holy temple; the LORD's throne is in heaven; His eyes behold, His eyelids test the sons of men. The LORD tests the righteous and the wicked, and the one who loves violence His soul hates. Upon the wicked He will rain snares; fire and brimstone and burning wind will be the portion of their cup" (Ps. 11:4–6). Here, we learn that the wicked are the object of divine hatred and rejection. Those who are unredeemed cannot approach God in His holy temple. David asserts that because God is absolutely holy, He hates all that is unholy. In the same way, He loves all that is in conformity with His own holiness.

Again, David establishes the truth that holy God is opposed to those who are sinful in His sight: "The face of the LORD is against evildoers, to cut off the memory of them from the earth" (Ps. 34:16). This means His foes will be so utterly defeated that they will be soon forgotten. They will never enter the presence of holy God in their sin-stained impurity.

The whole purpose of the sacrificial system was to teach that holy God is inaccessible by sinful man. The Levitical system was established by God to show that a priest must bring a sacrifice to God on behalf of the people. It was designed to teach that He cannot be approached by sinful creatures as they are. There must be a mediator to stand between God and man. God is too holy to look upon sinful creatures with acceptance. Paul writes that God "dwells in unapproachable light, whom no man has seen or can see" (1 Tim. 6:16). He lives in blazing holiness in a realm that is far too pure for the impure to enter.

The sacrificial system pointed to Jesus, who would be both the perfect High Priest, who offered the perfect sacrifice to make the way for sinners to approach God. Because God is holy and cannot have fellowship with sinful man, "He made Him who knew no sin to be sin on our behalf, so that we might become the righteousness of God in Him" (2 Cor. 5:21). Christ made those for whom He died holy so that He might present them faultless before God.

GOD IS CONVICTING

Included in the holiness of God is the reality that He exposes all sin hidden in darkness. The apostle John records, "God is Light, and in Him there is no darkness at all" (1 John 1:5). This means God is without any shadow of evil within Him. As noted earlier, He is sinless, unsullied by even the least trace of sin. Being light itself, He shines His holiness into every dark place. He reveals all that is unholy in His creatures.

When Isaiah encountered the blazing light of the holiness of God, he became painfully convicted of his immense lack of holiness. In the light of God's perfect purity, his own impurity was immediately and painfully exposed. He said, "I am a man of unclean lips, and I live among a people of unclean lips" (Isa. 6:5). In this dramatic confrontation, he became unusually aware of the depravity of his own sinful heart and lips. He saw himself as he had never seen himself before. As long as he compared himself with those around him, Isaiah remained relatively comfortable. But when he saw himself in light of God's holiness, he saw more of himself than he could bear.

Moreover, Isaiah suddenly became overwhelmed by the sinful condition of the nation. Upon seeing God, he was made grievously aware of the prevalent arrogance, envy, and materialism in the surrounding culture. The corrupt society in which he lived came sharply into focus because "my eyes have seen the King, the LORD of hosts" (v. 5). Such an encounter with divine holiness shook him to the core of his being. As a sinful creature, he found it personally devastating to gaze upon the holiness of God.

This same confrontation with divine holiness devastated Peter. After the miraculous catch of fish in Luke, he suddenly came to the realization that he was standing in the presence of impeccable holiness incarnate. He responded, "Go away from me Lord, for I am a sinful man!" (Luke 5:8). As he stood face-to-face with such perfect holiness, Peter suddenly became aware of his own sinfulness. This convicted disciple requested that Jesus withdraw from him lest he be ruined. It was more than he could bear.

The same devastating realization struck John on the island of Patmos. This last living apostle heard a loud voice, like a clap of thunder from heaven, speaking behind him. When he turned to see the One who was addressing him, John saw the glorified Christ in His unfiltered holiness. Among other features, he beheld that "His face was like the sun shining in its strength" (Rev. 1:16). Standing before the Holy One, John "fell at His feet like a dead man" (v. 17). In the presence of a holy and convicting God, He lost his senses. He collapsed, unconscious, to the ground.

SEEK HOLINESS

The holiness of God is the standard that every believer must pursue. God says: "For I am the LORD your God. Consecrate yourselves therefore, and be holy, for I am holy" (Lev. 11:44). God reinforces this charge to pursue personal holiness a second time: "You shall be holy, for I am holy" (v. 45). Again, "You shall be holy, for I the LORD your God am holy" (19:2; cf. 20:26). God calls His people to live in a distinctly different way from the sin-indulging lifestyles of the world. Here, He rejoices that they live in separation from sin in their hearts and external actions. The basis of holy living is the perfect holy character of God Himself.

One defining mark of every true believer is the pursuit of personal holiness. This is a necessary trait in the life of every true believer. The author of Hebrews writes, "Pursue . . . the sanctification without which no one will see the Lord" (Heb. 12:14). Every believer has a moral responsibility before God to expend effort in pursuing sanctification, which is greater growth in holiness. The believer must be continually turning away from sin, resisting the devil, and fleeing temptation. He must always keep himself unstained from the defilements of the world.

He must make every effort to live a holy life. Peter writes, "As obedient children, do not be conformed to the former lusts which were yours in your ignorance, but like the Holy One who called you, be holy yourselves also in all your behavior; because it is written, 'You shall be holy, for I am holy'" (1 Peter 1:14–16). As God is holy, so must we be holy, because He has made us to be "a holy priesthood" (2:5). Every aspect of our lives must be marked by a true seeking after holiness, by seeking after this Holy One.

Chapter Eight

ETERNALLY UNCHANGING

The Immutability of God

God cannot change for the better, for He is perfect;
and being perfect, He cannot change for the worse.

—A.W. PINK

Wherever Christianity has the strongest and deepest roots, there it cultivates the highest view of God. Like a towering oak tree, no church or movement can stand taller than the depth of its roots in knowledge of God's character. The same is true for any individual believer. A profound understanding of God inevitably leads to towering worship. An awesome vision of God enlarges hearts to greater love for Him and encourages the development of our souls to soar to the heights of heaven. A transcendent view of the character of God prompts lives to pursue what is pleasing to Him. Just as a healthy root system is vital for a mighty oak tree to grow, the roots of our knowledge of God must be deep and solid. The knowledge of God is, simply, that pivotal in the life of the church and every believer.

This reality makes the focus of this chapter so vitally important. An understanding of the immutability of God is critical to having an exalted view of Him. Immutability is drawn from the Latin word *immutabilis*, meaning "unchangeable." This is the crucial truth that God never changes in His person, plan, or purpose. Though this world is constantly changing, He remains fixed, forever the same. Society's fluctuating values and fashions are ever changing, but God remains unalterable. This divine attribute of immutability makes God the one permanent reality in the midst of an always oscillating universe.

It is impossible for God to change, either for the better or the worse. If God changed for the better, it would mean that He is presently imperfect. If God changed for the worse, it would mean He would become imperfect. However, God is constant in who He is, forever the same in His perfections. He never diminishes. He never differs in any of His eternal attributes.

GOD IS NEVER-CHANGING

The best starting place is with the truth that God is unchanging in His eternal being. Samuel said, "The Glory of Israel will not lie or change His mind; for He is not a man that He should change His mind" (1 Sam. 15:29). "The Glory of Israel" is a unique name for God that means He alone is the glory of His people. God is eternally the same in His character and word. Though man is constantly changing his mind, God never alters His eternal purposes or plans. Every one of His divine perfections is unalterable. This makes God entirely unlike His creation. We are never the same, always fluctuating in our physical and mental strength. As we grow older, we increase in wisdom and holiness, but experience physical deterioration. We can even suffer loss of memory. But God remains immutable, forever the same in His brilliance and strength.

The psalmist declares this same truth: "Even they will perish, but You endure; and all of them will wear out like a garment; like clothing You will change them and they will be changed. But You are the same, and Your years will not come to an end" (Ps. 102:26–27). Everything created by God is changing and perishing. But God, the Creator, never changes. Neither will He ever come to an end. Moreover, the psalmist affirms that the love of God for His own people is unchanging: "But the lovingkindness of the LORD is from everlasting to everlasting on those who fear Him" (Ps. 103:17). God is fixed and steadfast in His unchanging devotion toward His chosen ones. God Himself says, "For I, the LORD, do not change; therefore you, O sons of Jacob, are not consumed" (Mal. 3:6). God proclaims He is unalterable in His divine being. He remains the same from one generation to the next.

The New Testament reinforces this truth of divine immutability by applying the same verses from the Psalms to Jesus Christ (Heb. 1:10–12). Further, the writer of Hebrews testifies concerning Christ, "Jesus Christ is the same yesterday and today and forever" (13:8). From generation to generation, Jesus is the same in every aspect of His being. James says, "Every good thing given and every perfect gift is from above, coming down from the Father of lights, with whom there is no variation or shifting shadow" (James 1:17). There is no alteration in the character of God—His holiness, omnipotence, and wisdom are enduring constants.

GOD IS SELF-CONSISTENT

Another aspect of the immutability of God is that He is always consistent with His word. Balaam rightly says, "God is not a man, that He should lie, nor a son of man, that He should repent; has He said, and will He not do it? Or has He spoken, and will He not make it good?" (Num. 23:19). God will never take back something He has said. God never needs to amend His statements about any matter. All He has spoken in His Word stands true forever. He will never say one thing and later revise it. No word that proceeds from Him can be altered. What God has spoken is permanent, as if it were etched in stone with a pen of iron. His word will never fail to come to pass. Even the best people have changed what they said. But such wavering can never be ascribed to God.

The psalmist gives a strong testimony to the unchangeableness of the Word of God: "Forever, O LORD, Your word is settled in heaven" (Ps. 119:89). This declares the Word of God is forever fixed and remains firm. His Word does not morph with the shifting times in which we live. It is not altered according to what the whims of society dictate. What God says is utterly reliable from one generation to the next.

Confirming this very point, Jesus says, "For truly I say to you, until heaven and earth pass away, not the smallest letter or stroke shall pass from the Law until all is accomplished" (Matt. 5:18). "The smallest letter" in the Hebrew alphabet is a *yod*, a minuscule mark that looks like a small apostrophe. The smallest "stroke" is a *tittle*, a tiny line protruding from a Hebrew letter that distinguishes it from another letter. A tittle is similar to a serif with feet that differentiates a lowercase *i* in our English alphabet from a lowercase *t*. Every truth spoken by God—down to the smallest letter and stroke—will be brought to complete fulfillment.

Jesus further underscores the permanence of His Word when He says, "It is easier for heaven and earth to pass away than for one stroke of a letter of the Law to fail" (Luke 16:17). By this emphatic statement, Jesus maintains that it would be easier for the whole universe to disappear from existence than for one letter of the Word of God to fail to be accomplished. What God said yesterday will be true today and well into tomorrow. What the Bible declares to be right today will be right tomorrow. What God says is now wrong will be wrong forever. From one century to the next, the moral standard set by God never shifts. The Word of God remains the same for every people throughout time.

GOD IS ROCK-SOLID

One analogy used in Scripture to picture the immutability of God is the image of a sturdy rock. This metaphor describes God as the "rock" (Hebrew *tsur*), which portrays Him not as a little pebble or stone, but as an enormous mountain of strength. "Behold, I will stand before you there on the rock at Horeb; and you shall strike the rock, and water will come out of it, that the people may drink" (Ex. 17:6). "Then the LORD said, 'Behold, there is a place by Me, and you shall stand there on the rock; and it will come about, while My glory is passing by, that I will put you in the cleft of the rock and cover you with My hand until I have passed by'" (Ex. 33:21–22).

Moses says, "The Rock! His work is perfect, for all His ways are just" (Deut. 32:4). He chided the Lord's people, saying, "You neglected the Rock who begot you, and forgot the God who gave you birth" (v. 18). Because His people turned to false gods, Moses says, "Indeed their rock is not like our Rock" (v. 31). Any other object of trust is a faux hope, a false fortress. Only God is stable and enduring. He alone is the fixed constant in the midst of changing times. Unlike water that is ever moving, unstable, and taking the path of least resistance, God is our Rock, who never moves, never changes, and instead causes others to change.

David praises God, "The LORD is my rock and my fortress and my deliverer; my God, my rock, in whom I take refuge, my shield and the horn of my salvation, my stronghold and my refuge; my savior, You save me from violence" (2 Sam. 22:2–3). "For who is God, besides the LORD? And who is a rock, besides our God?" (v. 32). This depiction of God as a rock is intended to show that He is solid and steady, not subject to change. Unlike shifting sand, God is a rock, not blown about by the howling winds of change.

Frequently in the Psalms, David again references God as his rock: "The LORD is my rock and my fortress and my deliverer, my God, my rock, in whom I take refuge" (Ps. 18:2). Once more, David praises God, "O LORD, my rock and my Redeemer" (Ps. 19:14). David sees God as unchanging like a solid rock. He is not like a leaf or blade of grass that changes its colors. He is not like an animal that sheds its fur. God is like an immovable boulder, never changing and always the same.

David also writes, "He only is my rock and my salvation, my stronghold; I shall not be greatly shaken" (Ps. 62:2). David can remain strong even in uncertain times because God is strong and secure like a rock, never changing in composition or position. He adds, "He only is my rock and my salvation, my stronghold; I shall not be shaken. On God my salvation and my glory rest; the rock of my strength, my refuge is in God" (vv. 6–7).

GOD IS STRONG-WILLED

The immutability of God necessitates that His sovereign will, foreordained in eternity past, is unchanging. His eternal decree, predetermined before the foundation of the world, can never be altered by the will of man. The psalmist writes, "The LORD nullifies the counsel of the nations; He frustrates the plans of the peoples. The counsel of the LORD stands forever, the plans of His heart from generation to generation" (Ps. 33:10–11). The counsel of the nations will be brought to nothing. The plans of earthly monarchs, ruling over their nations, bow to the unalterable sovereign will of God.

The most powerful man in his hour of history, Solomon, acknowledges, "Many plans are in a man's heart, but the counsel of the LORD will stand" (Prov. 19:21). Even the king over Israel confesses that despite his plans, God's eternal purpose moves forward. God never shifts to plan B. Human plans can never cause God to redirect His absolute sovereign will. God has had only one plan, plan A, from before time began. No occurrence in the world can overturn the good that God has planned for His people.

The prophet Isaiah affirmed that none can thwart what God has purposed: "This is the plan devised against the whole earth; and this is the hand that is stretched out against all the nations. For the LORD of hosts has planned, and who can frustrate it? And as for His stretched-out hand, who can turn it back?" (Isa. 14:26–27). These rhetorical questions demand a negative answer. God's eternal plan inevitably moves forward exactly as He has purposed it. God will bring about the completion of His will exactly as He predetermined it in eternity past.

GOD IS EVER-SAVING

Because God is immutable, He is ever-saving in the exercise of His rescuing grace. In eternity past, God chose His elect and gave them to His Son to be His chosen bride. Before the world was created, He predestined the salvation of these chosen individuals whom He purposed to bring into His presence. God gave these elect ones to His Son, who came into this world and secured their salvation through His substitutionary death. The regenerating work of the Holy Spirit births these same elect into God's family. The Spirit grants them repentance and saving faith. These same chosen ones will be kept secure in the faith, forever in right standing with God. From eternity past to eternity future, His sovereign purpose in saving grace remains steadfast. No believer will ever become an unbeliever. No one adopted into the family of God will be expelled. No one who enters the kingdom will ever be cast out and become an exile.

Paul clearly stated the unchangeableness of God in His saving purposes, writing, "Those whom He foreknew, He also predestined to become conformed to the image of His Son, so that He would be the firstborn among many brethren; and these whom He predestined, He also called; and these whom He called, He also justified; and these whom He justified, He also glorified" (Rom. 8:29–30). These are the five unbreakable links in God's golden chain of salvation. Those whom He foreknew and predestined in eternity past are those whom God calls and justifies within time. It is these whom He glorifies in eternity future. No one else is added to this remnant within time. Likewise, no one falls away from His grace. Those whom God chose before time are those whom He will glorify when time is no more.

The apostle John equates salvation with receiving eternal life. Jesus teaches, "For God so loved the world, that He gave His only begotten Son, that whoever believes in Him shall not perish, but have eternal life" (John 3:16). "Eternal life" (Greek *zōē aiōnios*) means, literally, "the life of the ages to come." In the new birth, God implants divine life into the spiritually dead soul. Eternal life describes both the quality and duration of this life. God gives a quality of life that comes down from heaven itself and is unlike anything the world can give. Moreover, eternal life speaks to the duration of this new life in Christ. He bestows eternal life that continues forever. God does not give spiritual life that ebbs and flows, or comes and goes, because He never changes.

Jesus said that he who believes in Him "shall never thirst" (John 4:14; cf. 6:35). This means he will be forever satisfied in the Lord Jesus Christ. The one who believes in Him "has" (present tense) "eternal life" (John 5:24). This speaks to the unchangeable nature of God's saving purposes. Every believer will be "raise[d] . . . up on the last day" (John 6:40). Jesus said he will "never perish" (John 10:28) and "never die" (John 11:26). This lasting salvation is guaranteed by the constancy of God Himself.

Jesus told His disciples that the Holy Spirit will "be with you forever" (John 14:16). These words of Jesus Christ clearly affirm the irrevocable purposes of God in salvation. The apostle Paul writes, "For I am confident of this very thing, that He who began a good work in you will perfect it until the day of Christ Jesus" (Phil. 1:6). Here is the perseverance of the saints, which is, in reality, the perseverance of God in the saints.

GOD IS SELF-CONTROLLED

Because God is unchanging, He is, therefore, not subject to any fluctuating emotions provoked by the actions of His creatures. People do not have the power to disturb God. They cannot make Him more joyful or upset. This is known as the impassivity of God, meaning He cannot be emotionally controlled or manipulated by mankind. Put another way, God is without mood swings. Though He has affections, God is emotionally stable, incapable of being swayed by any external force. Impassivity means God cannot be changed in His feelings by anything that is inflicted on Him by mankind. He is unflappable and unfazed. Otherwise, God would not be immutable.

For God to be impassive, though, does not mean He is without affections. He is not a mere stoic Sovereign, nor a robotic Redeemer without feelings. To the contrary, the Scripture states that God grieves (Gen. 6:6), feels anger (Num. 11:1), rejoices (Isa. 62:5), and is full of compassion (Rom. 9:15). He clearly does have emotions. Yet, God is not governed by anything outside Himself. His inner life is not controlled by the sinful acts or tragedies of a fallen world. He remains self-controlled, even as all creation and circumstances are controlled by Him. God has affections, but not passions in the sense that He is passive and is made subject to the actions of His creatures. God is always the initiator of all things, never the responder. He is the unmoved Mover. So as it is, God remains immutable and sovereign over His affections.

GOD IS MERCIFULLY ACCOMMODATING

Included in the immutability of God is the truth that He never changes His mind. However, admittedly, there are selected verses in Scripture that seem to indicate otherwise. In the days before the flood, the Bible records, "The LORD was sorry that He had made man on the earth, and He was grieved in His heart. The LORD said, 'I will blot out man whom I have created from the face of the land, from man to animals to creeping things and to birds of the sky; for I am sorry that I have made them'" (Gen. 6:6–7). How do we reconcile these passages with the immutability of God? Man's sin truly grieved God's heart, because He is absolutely holy in His nature. But it was man who changed, not God. In reality, God chooses to reveal Himself in an accommodating way to man. This way, finite man can come closer to understanding the infinite nature of God.

On another occasion, God's people fall into gross idolatry during their forty-year journey through the wilderness. The Bible says, "So the LORD changed His mind about the harm which He said He would do to His people" (Ex. 32:14). "Changed His mind" (Hebrew *naham*) could be translated as "was sorry" or "was moved with pity." Moses appeals to God to change His mind in judging Israel, and God responds with genuine compassion. From man's perspective, God changed His mind. But from the divine perspective, God did what He had always eternally purposed to do. There was no alteration to the immutable will of God. These passages and many more (e.g., 1 Sam. 15:11–29; Jonah 3:10) actually express God's unalterable holiness, not any changeability on His part. Man's sin sorrows God's heart. God "changed His mind" because He was grieved by man's sin. This self-revelation by God is to accommodate man's weakness in understanding Him, not indicating any true change in His character or purpose.

OUR STRONG CONFIDENCE

As we live surrounded by a constantly changing world, we should take great confidence that God is never changing. Though society is in a constant state of change, God is not fluctuating in His being or purposes. He is forever the same. Though culture is unraveling before our eyes, God is the one fixed constant in our lives. He alone is the Rock of refuge upon whom our lives rest—forever stable and secure.

Though surrounded by such instability, we can move forward with renewed hope that God is the same throughout the ages to come. He is unalterable in His eternal being, the same throughout all our days. He never changes to be something other than the whole of what we first knew Him to be. We will never need to rescind our original commitment to Him because He has switched His plans or promises.

Because God never changes, our hope remains strong. We are confident because our God endures as we first knew Him. The immutability of God means our faith remains anchored to our Rock, who is steadfast and sure. Though the winds of this age blow, the object of our trust remains the same—forever.

Chapter Nine

UNIVERSALLY PRESENT

The Omnipresence of God

*God is an infinite circle whose center is everywhere
and whose circumference is nowhere.*

—AUGUSTINE OF HIPPO

One of the most mind-stretching truths about God is His omnipresence. This astonishing attribute speaks to the reality that He is everywhere present, every moment, with the fullness of His entire being. This truth defies our human capacity to comprehend it. Our finite minds simply cannot grasp this infinite dimension of His divine nature. We try to apprehend this omnipresent God, but we cannot completely comprehend Him. Attempting to fit this aspect of God into our small minds is like trying to pour the bottomless ocean into a tiny thimble—it simply will not fit.

Though this divine attribute of His omnipresence is beyond our understanding, we nevertheless must seek to understand what we can about God. Eternal life is knowing Him in a personal relationship. Jesus says, "This is eternal life, that they may know You, the only true God, and Jesus Christ whom You have sent" (John 17:3). Those who are born again enter into this experiential knowledge of God. But this encounter is only an initial introduction into knowing Him. From that moment forward, we are called to "grow in the grace and knowledge of our Lord and Savior Jesus Christ" (2 Peter 3:18).

Granted, we will never discover all the depths of who God is. That would be impossible, and to presume that such a feat is within our grasp would be sheer folly. But we can grow to know Him deeper and closer as He reveals Himself to us in His Word. We will never fully grasp Him, but we can explore His magnificent deeps. In this chapter, we will examine one such jewel found in these fathomless caverns—the omnipresence of God.

GOD IS EVERYWHERE

The theological term *omnipresence* begins with the Latin prefix *omni,* which means "all." God is all-present within His universe, with the whole of His being. There is no place within the created order from which God is excluded—not in heaven, on the earth, or below it. As discussed in an earlier chapter, God is a spirit being without a physical body (John 4:24). As a spirit, He is without any spatial limitations. Being without a corporeal substance or form, He is not confined to a single location. Thus, God can be present everywhere at the same time.

David recognizes the omnipresence of God when he asks this rhetorical question, "Where can I go from Your Spirit?" (Ps. 139:7). This clearly implies the negative answer that there is nowhere God does not exist. David then asks a second question:

"Or where can I flee from Your presence?" (v. 7). This anticipates the same negative answer. There is nowhere that God is not present. David further explains: "If I ascend to heaven, You are there; if I make my bed in Sheol, behold, You are there. If I take the wings of the dawn, if I dwell in the remotest part of the sea, even there Your hand will lead me, and Your right hand will lay hold of me" (vv. 8–10). "Heaven" is due north, while "Sheol" is the grave or, metaphorically, south. "The dawn" is where the sun rises in the east. "The sea" is a reference to the Mediterranean Sea, which is to the west of the Holy Land.

No matter where David goes—north, south, east, or west—God is already there. When David goes to heaven, God dwells there. When he dies, God is on the other side of the grave, waiting for him. Whether he travels to the east or to the west, God is already there. No matter where David goes, God is present. In fact, God is so close that wherever he goes, His hand still rests on David. There is no possible location where he can escape from the omnipresence of God.

Whether in life or death, time or eternity, God is there with the fullness of His being. His presence cannot be contained in any one place of the universe. Nor can He be excluded from any part within it. Paul writes, there is "one God and Father of all who is over all and through all and in all" (Eph. 4:6). Those prepositional phrases—*of* all, *over* all, *through* all, *in* all—teach us that whether in heaven, on earth, or under the earth, God is all-present.

To be clear, the manifestation of His divine presence is not the same everywhere. God is revealed far more directly in heaven than He is on the earth. Likewise, there are places on the earth where His glory is more fully revealed than at other sites. For example, His presence at the burning bush was made known far more dramatically than it was in the midst of idolatrous Egypt. His presence in the Holy of Holies of the temple was manifested more vividly than it is in the flames of hell. Nevertheless, He is still equally present at each of these places at all times.

GOD IS EXALTED

The Bible specifically teaches that God dwells in the heights of heaven above. The psalmist states that God "sits in the heavens" (Ps. 2:4). He occupies the highest place of supreme authority in the heavens. The word "heavens" (Hebrew *shamayim*) literally means "heights." In this psalm, "heavens" is in the plural, meaning God is in the loftiest heights of heaven. David explains, "The LORD is in His holy temple; the LORD's throne is in heaven" (Ps. 11:4). He fills every corner of heaven with the fullness of His majestic presence.

The psalmist declares, "For You are the LORD Most High over all the earth" (Ps. 97:9). Exalted in heaven, God towers over all creation in the highest parts of heaven as the "Most High." The psalmist says, "The LORD has established His throne in the heavens" (Ps. 103:19). There, God sits enthroned above. Again, the psalmist declares, "You who are enthroned in the heavens!" (Ps. 123:1). Solomon states, "God is in heaven" (Eccl. 5:2). Isaiah adds, God is "the high and exalted One," who dwells "on a high and holy place" (Isa. 57:15). Even God Himself states His lofty location: "Heaven is My throne" (Isa. 66:1). God presides over the affairs of this world from atop the greatest heights of heaven.

In the Sermon on the Mount, Jesus said "heaven" is where "the throne of God" is (Matt. 5:34). When we pray, He instructs us to approach God this way: "Our Father who is in heaven" (Matt. 6:9). When Jesus rebuked the Pharisees, He said, "And whoever swears by heaven, swears both by the throne of God and by Him who sits upon it" (Matt. 23:22). He recognized that God is established upon His throne in heaven. When the apostle John was exiled on the island of Patmos, he heard a voice saying, "Come up here" (Rev. 4:1). A door was opened in heaven, and he was caught up in his spirit to enter it. As we previously noted, what immediately captured his attention was "a throne [that] was standing in heaven, and One sitting on the throne" (v. 2). He saw a staggering sight—God, enthroned on high, filling heaven with the fullness of His presence.

GOD IS BEYOND

Further, God fills the vastness of outer space with His entire presence. With His mighty right hand, He upholds the sun, moon, and planets in their place—for billions of galaxies. Job recognized that God "alone stretches out the heavens" (Job 9:8; cf. Ps. 104:2). Elihu asked Job, "Can you, with Him, spread out the skies, strong as a molten mirror?" (Job 37:18). Only God can handcraft the skies and all they contain, and only He can keep them in their assigned place.

God asked Job, "Can you bind the chains of the Pleiades, or loose the cords of Orion? Can you lead forth a constellation in its season, and guide the Bear with her satellites?" (Job 38:31–32). Pleiades and Orion are stellar constellations in expansive space above. "The Bear" is perhaps a reference to the constellation known as Ursa Major. The obvious answer to these questions is that Job cannot control these starry hosts. Only God can govern the countless stars. Again, God quizzed Job, "Who can . . . tip

111

the water jars of the heavens?" (v. 37). In other words, who could cause the rain to fall? Only God, who dwells in the skies above, can control this phenomenon. In every corner of the known— and unknown—universe, God is perfectly present.

GOD IS IMMEDIATE

God is also present everywhere on our tiny planet: the Earth. Solomon declared: "But will God indeed dwell on the earth? Behold, heaven and the highest heaven cannot contain You" (1 Kings 8:27). The fascinating answer to Solomon's question is yes, God does live on the earth. His transcendent glory fills both the heights of heaven and this mortal world. God is not only present far away, but He is also immanently near. The fullness of His divine presence permeates the whole earth. Rahab says, "He is God in heaven above and on earth beneath" (Josh. 2:11). God is equally present on the earth as He is in heaven. He is not more in heaven than on the earth. Granted, there are places where His presence is more greatly and clearly manifested than in other places. But He is equally present everywhere.

When the Tower of Babel was built, it was a pitiful attempt by feeble man to reach the heights of heaven. In response, God said, "Come, let Us go down" (Gen. 11:7). This descent by God was an anthropomorphism, indicating God's special presence and activity on the earth in humanlike terms. In the days of Sodom and Gomorrah, God said, "I will go down now, and see if they have done entirely according to its outcry" (Gen. 18:21). Again, this divine descent was intended to indicate God's activity on the earth. When God gave the Ten Commandments, "the LORD came down on Mount Sinai" (Ex. 19:20). This means that God acted in a special way on the mountain. The same descent by God later occurred before Moses: "The LORD descended in the cloud and stood there with him" (Ex. 34:5). It was then that God gave a greater self-revelation to Moses.

Moses reaffirms this truth that God is near when he says, "He is God in heaven above and on the earth below" (Deut. 4:39). God is able to simultaneously occupy both the heavenly and earthly realms with the fullness of His presence. David took great comfort in this truth: "Even though I walk through the valley of the shadow of death, I fear no evil, for You are with me" (Ps. 23:4). David had the consoling assurance that wherever he went and whatever he faced in life, he was never alone. Even in the dark valley of death, God was with him. Through the prophet Isaiah, God said, "Heaven is My throne and the earth is My footstool" (Isa. 66:1). The fullness of God fills the whole earth, yet He mysteriously dwells with the "humble and contrite of spirit" (v. 2). God draws near to His people when they are in the lowest places on the earth. He is especially with those who are bowed down, even broken down. At the same time, He is present to oppose the proud (James 4:6).

The Lord asks: "'Am I a God who is near,' declares the LORD, 'and not a God far off? . . . Do I not fill the heavens and the earth?'" (Jer. 23:23–24). The seemingly paradoxical point is that God is in heaven *and* on the earth, far away *and* near. Even so, as the disciples would go into the nations, Jesus promised, "I am with you always, even to the end of the age" (Matt. 28:20). There are no territorial restrictions to His divine omnipresence.

GOD IS INWARD

God is also uniquely present within all believers. Jesus Christ promises His disciples that "the Spirit of truth . . . will be in you"

(John 14:17). Despite His return to the Father, He assures them of His abiding presence within them: "I in you" (v. 20). Jesus again pledges His indwelling presence: "I in you" (15:4). In fact, the Father also lives within believers. Jesus says, "We will come to him and make Our abode with him" (14:23). When Jesus prays to the Father, He describes Himself as "I in them" (17:23).

This inward presence of Jesus Christ within believers is made real via the person of the Holy Spirit. To believers, Paul states, "The Spirit of God dwells in you" (Rom. 8:9). "Christ is in you" (v. 10). "The Spirit of Him who raised Jesus from the dead dwells in you" (v. 11). "Your body is a temple of the Holy Spirit who is in you" (1 Cor. 6:19). The apostle Paul taught that "Christ lives in me" (Gal. 2:20). Though we were once alienated from God, we have been brought into fellowship with Him through Christ. "You who formerly were far off have been brought near" to God (Eph. 2:13). God is so near that He indwells us. Paul prayed for believers that "Christ may dwell in your hearts" (Eph. 3:17). God the Father is "in all" (Eph. 4:6), including all believers. Paul writes, "Christ in you" (Col. 1:27).

God is with us in every circumstance of life—not only on the mountaintop but in the valleys of life. To His saints, He pledges, "I will never desert you, nor will I ever forsake you" (Heb. 13:5). He is never any closer to us than when we need Him the most. James assures us, "Draw near to God and He will draw near to you" (James 4:8). When the Bible says unbelievers are far away from God, it refers to a relational separation, not a spatial distance. They must come to God within their hearts, not by their feet to a certain location. They can never escape His presence.

GOD IS BELOW

Because there is no place where God does not exist, this must also include the depths of hell. If God is in the heights of heaven, He must likewise be present in the depths of the fiery pit. Though this may sound shocking, God is equally present in that awful place where there is "weeping and gnashing of teeth" (Matt. 8:12). God Himself is personally in hell, carrying out His vengeance on the ungodly. He is there in the fullness of His power, inflicting His relentless wrath on unrepentant sinners. Sinners are not administering their own eternal punishment. Neither is Satan doing the punishing of unbelievers, nor doing it to himself. Instead, this act of divine retribution is being executed by God, who is fully present in the outer darkness to do so.

In the flames of hell, unbelievers "drink of the wine of the wrath of God" (Rev. 14:10). It is God Himself who gives this cup of divine anger to reprobates in perdition. They will not voluntarily choose to drink from this foul cup. Rather, it will be forced on them by the Lord. John records that every unbeliever in hell "will be tormented with fire and brimstone in the presence of the holy angels and in the presence of the Lamb" (v. 10). This indicates that the unbelievers will be acted upon by someone else. This divine wrath will be unleashed on sinners in the immediate presence of the Lamb, Jesus Christ. This is to say, this eternal punishment is being inflicted by the Lord Himself, who is the executor of His own wrath in hell.

The presence of God in hell needs to be reconciled with other passages that might seem to indicate otherwise. For example, Paul writes, "These will pay the penalty of eternal destruction, away from the presence of the Lord and from the glory of His power"

(2 Thess. 1:9). In this verse, "presence" (Greek *prosōpon*) literally means "countenance, face." This means that the Lord will turn away His face from unbelievers. The favor of His countenance will be withdrawn. They will not experience the smile of His face in hell. Relationally separated from Him, they will nevertheless face the fierce frown of His anger. In their presence, God will unleash on them the endless execution of His vengeance. They will forever be the object of His unmitigated wrath, never to escape the divine fury of eternal destruction, as an outpouring of His justice.

A DOUBLE-EDGED BLADE

This truth of divine omnipresence is both comforting and convicting. Like a surgeon's knife, it cuts deeply both ways. It brings assurance to the heart, but it can also afflict the conscience. This doctrine can skillfully cut out sinful infections in our souls. It can also make an incision necessary for the spiritual healing of the heart.

This truth of the divine presence means we can never escape the presence of the Lord, no matter how hard we may try. As the prophet Jonah discovered, we cannot run away from God and His will. There are still people today who flee to another city or state to avoid obeying His purposed plan—by abandoning their spouse or their other divinely given commitments. They think they can avoid their accountability to the Lord by changing their location. But they soon realize that God is already there, waiting to deal with them. We cannot run away from Him who is omnipresent. God is present for every act that we ever commit. Though others may not be present to see the deed, God is always on site.

At the same time, the reality of this all-present God encourages those who find themselves in difficult situations. They realize that they are never alone, nor are they ever at a disadvantage. God plus one person always makes a majority. It is encouraging to know that God is with us in every adversity of life. In every difficulty, we are never left on our own. This all-present God is all-sufficient for us at all times. In all trials, He will never leave us nor forsake us.

We must allow our minds to be elevated and expanded by this truth of the omnipresence of God. We must have our hearts enlarged to soar to the heights of heaven with renewed trust in Him. When this reality about God grips our hearts, we will be humbled and give Him the praise He rightly deserves. We can never escape God—not in this life, nor in the one to come—a truth that is both convicting and comforting.

Chapter Ten

INTIMATELY KNOWING

The Omniscience of God

Though God is out of sight, we are not out of His sight.

—Matthew Henry

Having learned about the omnipresence of God, we now unearth the next precious gem in God's treasure vault—the subject of His omniscience. This attribute means God knows everything there is to know. He never learns anything. Nothing new ever enters His mind. He never looks down the tunnel of time to discover anything about the future He did not already know. He never receives a news update concerning something that had previously escaped His knowledge. Nothing ever catches Him off guard. God knows all of what will happen before it comes to pass. He knows what every outcome will be before it occurs. Simply put, nothing ever surprises Him.

The omniscience of God is a staggering truth that makes Him utterly incomprehensible to us. The apostle Paul exclaims: "Oh, the depth of the riches both of the wisdom and knowledge of

God! How unsearchable are His judgments and unfathomable His ways! For who has known the mind of the Lord, or who became His counselor?" (Rom. 11:33–34). These rhetorical questions are declarations of astonishment. The point Paul makes is that no one possesses any knowledge that God does not already know. Therefore, no one can possibly be His informant and give Him an insight He does not already possess.

In this chapter, we will examine the different aspects of the omniscience of God.

GOD IS ALL-KNOWING

The omniscience of God means He is entirely all-knowing. He knows everything actual and possible. He knows all matter and all matters. He sees into all thoughts, all desires, all feelings, and all choices. He perceives things visible and invisible as they really are. He understands all peoples and places. He has insight into all mysteries and secrets. He comprehends all principalities and powers, all thrones and dominions. He discerns all causes and all effects. Nothing escapes His knowledge.

Hannah confesses, "The LORD is a God of knowledge" (1 Sam. 2:3). Job asks, "Can anyone teach God knowledge?" (Job 21:22). The answer is that no one can bring to God any knowledge that He does not already possess. Elihu says that God is "One who is perfect in knowledge" (Job 36:4). Again, he maintains, God is "perfect in knowledge" (Job 37:16). The word "perfect" (Hebrew *tamim*) means "complete, whole, entire." God possesses a comprehensive knowledge of everything there is to know. Isaiah asks, "Who . . . taught Him knowledge and informed Him?" (Isa. 40:14). No one did, because God "knows all things" (1 John 3:20).

GOD IS SELF-KNOWING

The omniscience of God begins with the perfect knowledge that He possesses of His own infinite self. He is perfectly aware of every facet of His own being. He is fully informed about His own self-existence. He completely comprehends the full extent of His sovereignty and omnipotence. He exactly understands how and when everything He has decreed in eternity past will come to pass. He Himself knows that He rightly appraises His own attributes. He is well aware of what resources of wisdom and power He possesses. God has full knowledge of His own love and mercy toward His own people. He grasps the full extent of His righteousness and wrath. God knows Himself perfectly.

Moreover, each person of the Trinity knows the other persons eternally, intimately, and accurately. Jesus says, "No one knows the Son except the Father; nor does anyone know the Father except the Son, and anyone to whom the Son wills to reveal Him" (Matt. 11:27). Only Jesus, along with the Holy Spirit, truly knows what is the mind, heart, and will of God the Father. Likewise, only God the Father knows the Son and the Spirit. Jesus asserts, "The Father knows Me and I know the Father" (John 10:15). The Father possesses perfect knowledge of the Son, and the Son has perfect knowledge of the Father. Likewise, the Father and the Son perfectly know the Spirit, and the Spirit perfectly knows Them. The apostle Paul wrote, "The Spirit searches all things, even the depths of God" (1 Cor. 2:10). The inner-Trinitarian relationships between the divine members are personal and true.

The full knowledge within the Trinity of the other persons establishes the perfect unity between Them. Each person in the Trinity knows Their distinctive roles in carrying out the eternal decree of the Father. Each knows precisely what the other two persons are thinking, feeling, desiring, and choosing. Paul writes, "The thoughts of God no one knows except the Spirit of God" (1 Cor. 2:11). No one knows the depths of what God the Father knows except the Son and the Spirit. Such depths of self-knowledge belong equally and entirely to the three persons of the Godhead.

GOD IS ALL-FOREKNOWING

Beyond infinite self-knowledge, God knows everything that will come to pass. He knows what will happen in the future as well as He knows what happened in the past. From before the foundation of the world, He has known everything that will ever take place. He knows all things because He foreordained it all. God knows whatever will come to pass within time, because He decreed it before time began. As the Author of His eternal decree, He knows what will occur within the affairs of His providence.

With God, there is no succession of acquiring knowledge. As finite creatures, we grow increasingly in the accumulation of our knowledge. But this is not the case with God. He has known everything instantaneously from eternity past. He is never adding to His collective body of knowledge. God has always known everything that can be known—from the very beginning.

To this point, God says, "Remember the former things long past, for I am God, and there is no other; I am God, and there is no one like Me" (Isa. 46:9). God then explains what distinguishes Him from His creation and all false gods. He states, "I am God, and there is no one like Me, declaring the end from the beginning, and from ancient times things which have not been done" (vv.

9–10). God stood at the beginning of time and looked all the way to the end. From the outset, He declared everything that would occur until the end. Therefore, He knew all that would transpire because He had predetermined it all.

GOD IS ALL-SEEING

The Bible represents God as seeing everything that exists in the universe. This is one of the first truths about God revealed in the Bible. After each day of creation, God saw what He made and declared it was good. "God saw that the light was good" (Gen. 1:4). After He gathered the waters into one place, "God saw that it was good" (v. 10). The same was true with the following days of creation: "God saw that it was good" (vv. 18, 21, 25, 31). God perfectly sees all His works. Because He sees them, He knows them thoroughly.

Hagar illustrated this truth through a name she gave God when He spoke to her before Ishmael's birth—*El-Roi,* meaning "God who sees." Being an outcast, she was astonished that God saw her and took notice of her. "Then she called the name of the LORD who spoke to her, 'You are a God who sees'" (Gen. 16:13). This divine theophany led her to call Him "God who sees me," because nothing escapes His notice, not even the birth of Ishmael, an unwanted child. The well where this revelation of God occurred was named Beer-lahai-roi, which means "the well of the Living One who sees me" (v. 14). Because God sees all, He therefore knows all. God peers into the depths of what no man can see.

Hanni the prophet announces, "For the eyes of the LORD move to and fro throughout the earth that He may strongly support those whose heart is completely His" (2 Chron. 16:9). Here is another anthropomorphic expression that reveals God as having eyes that are all-seeing. Though God does not have physical eyes, He nevertheless does see and know all. God always sees the person whose heart is firmly committed to Him, wherever on the globe they may be. God is ever observing the path a man takes. Zophar rightly says, "He sees iniquity without investigating" (Job 11:11). Job adds, "His eyes are on their ways" (24:23). He states, "For He looks to the ends of the earth and sees everything under the heavens" (28:24). Job asks, "Does He not see my ways and number all my steps?" (31:4). This question is, in reality, a conclusive statement. God sees so perfectly that He can measure the smallest step of the most obscure person on the earth.

The psalmist wrote, "The LORD looks from heaven; He sees all the sons of men; from His dwelling place He looks out on all the inhabitants of the earth" (Ps. 33:13–14). No individual escapes His all-seeing gaze. David adds, "Your eyes have seen my unformed substance" (Ps. 139:16). "If I say, 'Surely the darkness will overwhelm me, and the light around me will be night,' even the darkness is not dark to You, and the night is as bright as the day. Darkness and light are alike to You" (vv. 11–12). God sees as clearly in the dark as He sees in the light. His penetrating vision in both the light and the darkness are alike to Him.

Solomon affirms the all-seeing eyes of God: "For the ways of a man are before the eyes of the LORD, and He watches all his paths" (Prov. 5:21). Every step a man takes is noted by God. Solomon writes, "The eyes of the LORD are in every place, watching the evil and the good" (Prov. 15:3). This means that God sees everyone and everything in every place. Nothing escapes His penetrating gaze. He sees the evil, the good, and everything morally neutral. God said: "My eyes are on all their ways; they are not hidden from My face" (Jer. 16:17). God asked, "Can a man hide himself in hiding places so I do not see him?" (Jer. 23:24). The answer to this question is an emphatic no. No one can hide from the sight of God.

GOD IS ALL-PERCEIVING

God perfectly understands all that He observes. He not only sees everything, but He sees through it. He sees into the depth of everything for the reality of what it really is. He not only sees the action, but the deep-seated motive behind it. He said to Samuel, "God sees not as man sees, for man looks at the outward appearance, but the LORD looks at the heart" (1 Sam. 16:7). Unlike mere man, God sees through the external human facade into the internal attitude. Elihu stated: "For His eyes are upon the ways of a man, and He sees all his steps. There is no darkness or deep shadow where the workers of iniquity may hide themselves. For He does not need to consider a man further, that he should go before God in judgment" (Job 34:21–23). In other words, there is no need for any witness to come to court before God. He already has full knowledge of all the evidence. In fact, the verdict has already been made.

The psalmist calls God "He who fashions the hearts of them all, He who understands all their works" (Ps. 33:15). Here, the psalmist states that God fully discerns all that He sees. "Understands" (Hebrew *bin*) means "to perceive, discern, distinguish." It can also mean "to be prudent, to regard." Thus, God discerns whatever He sees with perfect perception.

The psalmist declares, "His understanding is infinite" (Ps. 147:5). The word "understanding" (Hebrew *tebunah*) means "to comprehend what one sees." As earlier observed, the word "infinite" (Hebrew *ayin*) literally means "nothing" or "naught" and carries the idea that His understanding cannot even be numbered. There are no boundaries to the vast, immeasurable knowledge of God. What He comprehends is far beyond any calculation. He sizes up every person precisely as they truly are. He is never fooled by anyone. God never misreads any situation. He never misperceives the truth about anything.

The prophet Isaiah asked: "Who has directed the Spirit of the LORD, or as His counselor has informed Him? With whom did He consult and who gave Him understanding? And who taught Him in the path of justice and taught Him knowledge and informed Him of the way of understanding?" (Isa. 40:13–14). This series of rhetorical questions demands the same decisive answer—no one. God's understanding needs no additional insight or clarification from any earthly counselors.

GOD IS ALL-SCRUTINIZING

God knows every matter down to the smallest detail. Solomon confessed, "You alone know the hearts of all the sons of men" (1 Kings 8:39). God detects every detail of creation: "Do you know about the layers of the thick clouds, the wonders of one perfect in knowledge?" (Job 37:16).

In fact, God knows the exact number of the stars in outer space. The psalmist writes, "He counts the number of the stars; He gives names to all of them" (Ps. 147:4). The number of stars is unseen to the human eye and incalculable to the human mind. But not so with God. He knows their exact number and even gives them individual names.

God comprehends not only the big picture but also the most minute aspects. His vast knowledge enables Him to see the smallest details of every inconsequential circumstance taking place. Jesus said: "Are not two sparrows sold for a cent? And yet not one of them will fall to the ground apart from your Father. But the very hairs of your head are all numbered" (Matt. 10:29–30). At all times, God knows every bird in every tree of the world. Even when no one else is watching or caring, He knows when an otherwise unnoticed bird falls to the ground. He observes the most minuscule occurrence in each person's life. His knowledge extends to every individual hair on every head of the entire human race. The author of Hebrews writes, "And there is no creature hidden from His sight, but all things are open and laid bare to the eyes of Him with whom we have to do" (Heb. 4:13). None escapes His all-detecting gaze.

God sees through the outward veneer that we show to people around us. He peers into every corner of the human heart and examines their motives. God sifts through the secret places of every soul that lie hidden to men. The psalmist David exclaims, "O LORD, You have searched me and known me" (Ps. 139:1). The word "searched" (Hebrew *haqar*) means "to spy out, to dig deeply into a matter." It was used of the twelve spies going into the promised land to search out its terrain and enemies. As spies would explore a country, God examines every detail of our inner lives. Nothing escapes His all-inspecting stare. God probes the depths of every person's secret life.

In this same psalm, David added, "You know when I sit down and when I rise up" (v. 2). "Know" (*yada*) is the same Hebrew word that is used of the physical relationship between a husband and wife (Gen. 4:1, 17, 25). It means "to know someone intimately." In like manner, David writes that God is closely acquainted with him. The fact that God knows both his sitting down and rising up is a figure of speech known as inclusion. This literary device places these two activities on the opposite end of the spectrum and conveys that God knows the two extremes and everything in between. He knows every detail of our lives, from our rising up in the morning to our sitting down at night. God knows everything David does from sunrise to sunset. He is familiar with each of his activities over the course of the day.

David also says, "You understand my thought from afar" (Ps. 139:2). God plumbs the depths of his soul with a penetrating insight that discerns his private thoughts. David continues, "You scrutinize my path and my lying down" (v. 3). This word "scrutinize" (Hebrew *zarah*) means "to sift through something, to separate out." It was used of the practice of winnowing grain, separating the wheat from the tares, the good from the bad. God sorted through every thought David had and every step he took. God culled through the entirety of his life. David adds that God is "intimately acquainted with all my ways" (v. 3). Nothing he says or does escapes the internal audit of God. "Even before there is a word on my tongue, behold, O LORD, You know it all" (v. 4). God even knows what David will say before he thinks of what to say.

GOD IS ALL-REMEMBERING

Finally, God never forgets anything that He knows. Nothing ever limits His knowledge. He never fails to remember anything He previously knew. For example, God remembered His promise to Noah to protect him and the animals on the ark during the days of the flood: "But God remembered Noah and all the beasts and all the cattle that were with him in the ark" (Gen. 8:1). God did not forget His vow to preserve Noah and his family on board the ark. He remembered His covenant with His people forever. "And I will remember My covenant, which is between Me and you and every living creature of all flesh; and never again shall the water become a flood to destroy all flesh" (Gen. 9:15). No promise made by God will ever fade from His memory. His people can rest in His truth, knowing He will always keep His word.

In the days of Israel's Egyptian bondage, God remembered His longstanding covenant to make them a great nation: "So God heard their groaning; and God remembered His covenant with Abraham, Isaac, and Jacob" (Ex. 2:24). Despite the passing of time, nothing God promises ever slips His mind. Again, God said, "Furthermore I have heard the groaning of the sons of Israel, because the Egyptians are holding them in bondage, and I have remembered My covenant" (Ex. 6:5). Once more, God stated, "Then I will remember My covenant with Jacob, and I will remember also My covenant with Isaac, and My covenant with Abraham as well, and I will remember the land" (Lev. 26:42). Simply put, God never forgets anything He guarantees will come to pass.

These statements need to be reconciled with other passages in which God says He will not remember the sins of His people. God says, "I will not remember your sins" (Isa. 43:25). Again, God says, "I will forgive their iniquity, and their sin I will remember no more" (Jer. 31:34). In the New Testament, we read the same: "For I will be merciful to their iniquities, and I will remember their sins no more" (Heb. 8:12). Once more, "And their sins and their lawless deeds I will remember no more" (Heb. 10:17).

The explanation to this apparent contradiction is that though God certainly remembers our sins cognitively, He no longer remembers the sins of His people judicially. God, who forgets nothing, has chosen to remove our sins from us as far as the east is to the west (Ps. 103:12). All our sins are forgotten in their punishment, because Christ has satisfied the just penalty demanded by God.

A LIFE-CHANGING REALITY

This truth of divine omniscience is mind-boggling. It is encouraging to the believer to know that God knows us perfectly. When others misunderstand us and even misrepresent us, God nevertheless knows the truth about us. He knows when we have suffered unjustly for doing what is right. God knows when we have been falsely accused. Nothing escapes His notice. God sees every matter for what it truly is.

But at the same time, this truth also convicts us—and rightly so. Our Father knows every selfish motive of our hearts. He hears every unwholesome word we say. He perceives every motive behind what we do. God knows us with a depth of knowledge that would make us feel uncomfortable if another human knew us this way. Such truth should serve as a restraint in our lives from further sin.

This truth of God's omniscience will revolutionize our prayer life. When we pray to God, we are not informing Him of anything that He does not already know. We are not updating God as though He does not know what we are telling Him. Though He is engaged with every other matter in the universe, He is nevertheless preoccupied with our situation—as if nothing else is transpiring.

His undivided attention is always riveted on us. Nothing hinders His all-seeing gaze into our lives. He has all knowledge at His disposal and knows what is best for us.

What a marvelous truth—God knows us the best and still loves us the most. May this truth of divine omniscience have its sanctifying effect on our lives.

Chapter Eleven

IRRESISTIBLY POWERFUL

The Omnipotence of God

One Almighty is more than all mighties.

—WILLIAM GURNALL

Having considered that God is omnipresent and omniscient, we now turn our attention to a third divine attribute beginning with the Latin prefix *omni*. This truth is the omnipotence of God—the fact that He possesses all power. There is no power in the universe but that which belongs to Almighty God. His omnipotence means He is more than able to accomplish His sovereign will. There can be no successful resistance against His eternal purpose. Any lesser power used by His creatures is simply temporarily on loan from God. Everyone and everything derives its power from this one source—Almighty God.

If God is not omnipotent, He would not be able to accomplish His eternal will. God *must* be all-powerful to move everything forward to achieve His appointed end. Because God has all power, He can do any one thing as easily as He can do another thing.

It is all the same to God. Whatever He does is done effortlessly, because nothing is difficult for Him to carry out. When God acts, He loses none of His strength. He expends no energy that must be replenished. Because He is immutable, He never needs to regain any lost strength. His power always remains unchanged.

Given the greatness of God's power, we want to give careful thought to the different aspects of His irresistible might.

GOD IS ALL-POWERFUL

Since all of His attributes are infinite, God possesses unlimited power. His might is clearly seen in the first verse of the Bible: "In the beginning God created the heavens and the earth" (Gen. 1:1). This name for God (*Elohim*) is the plural form for God, known as a majestic plural. *El* is the Hebrew word for God, meaning "the strong One." This intensive plural identifies Him as the One who is all-mighty. The plural form indicates He has abundant power to accomplish His will.

Another Old Testament name for God is *El Shaddai*, which means "Almighty God." The Hebrew word *shaddai* means "mountain." This name for God pictures Him standing on a mountain as the Almighty One. It is how God appeared to Abram and announced, "I am God Almighty" (Gen. 17:1), the One who can fulfill His promises with ease. Isaac also called Him "God Almighty" (Gen. 28:3). God declared to Jacob, "I am God Almighty" (Gen. 35:11), the One who mightily makes all His purposes come to pass.

Job simply announces, "With Him [is] strength" (Job 12:16). When assailed by enemies, David pronounces, "Once God has spoken; twice I have heard this: that power belongs to God" (Ps.

62:11). There is no power but that which belongs to Him. God Himself says, "For thus says the LORD, who created the heavens (He is the God who formed the earth and made it, He established it and did not create it a waste place, but formed it to be inhabited), 'I am the LORD, and there is none else'" (Isa. 45:18). Here, *Elohim* is used again to reveal the all-powerful God who created all that exists.

In a satire against idolatry, Jeremiah declares the immense power of the true God: "There is none like You, O LORD; You are great, and great is Your name in might" (Jer. 10:6). Idols are altogether impotent, but the living God is all-powerful. Daniel praises God, saying: "Let the name of God be blessed forever and ever, for wisdom and power belong to Him" (Dan. 2:20). This profession declares that God, possessing all power, is the only One who grants might to men.

When on trial before the Jewish authorities, Jesus said, "You will see the Son of Man sitting at the right hand of Power, and coming on the clouds of heaven" (Matt. 26:64). "Power" is a simple but profound name to refer to God the Father, who is so powerful that He is identified by this attribute. In the New Testament, God is known in heaven as "the Almighty" (Rev. 4:8). This divine name means He is "Almighty" (Greek *pantokratōr*), the One who is irresistible in His power. He has the power to create and sustain all that He has made. He possesses the might to do whatever He pleases.

GOD IS ALL-CREATING

The power of God was vividly displayed in His act of creating the universe. He effortlessly spoke everything into being *ex nihilo*—out of nothing. The Bible states, "In the beginning God created the heavens and the earth" (Gen. 1:1). He dramatically made the universe without the slightest degree of difficulty. On Mount Sinai, God said, "For in six days the LORD made the heavens and the earth, the sea and all that is in them" (Ex. 20:11). God is so powerful that He created everything effortlessly in this brief amount of time.

The psalmist attributes to God the marvelous power of creation: "By the word of the LORD the heavens were made, and by the breath of His mouth all their host" (Ps. 33:6). God merely spoke and created the entire universe and all it contains without any difficulty whatsoever: "The heavens are Yours, the earth also is Yours; the world and all it contains, You have founded them. The north and the south, You have created them; Tabor and Hermon shout for joy at Your name. You have a strong arm; Your hand is mighty, Your right hand is exalted" (Ps. 89:11–13). The psalmist states, "Of old You founded the earth, and the heavens are the work of Your hands" (Ps. 102:25). This great omnipotence of God in creation is later ascribed to the Lord Jesus Christ in Hebrews 1:10–12.

God exclaimed, "Surely My hand founded the earth, and My right hand spread out the heavens; when I call to them, they stand together" (Isa. 48:13). The creation of the universe was like mere child's play for the Almighty. Jeremiah quotes God likewise: "I have made the earth, the men and the beasts which are on the face of the earth by My great power and by My outstretched arm" (Jer. 27:5). God extended His right arm, and the entire created order came into existence. Jeremiah repeated the same: "Ah Lord GOD! Behold, You have made the heavens and the earth by Your great power and by Your outstretched arm! Nothing is too difficult for You" (Jer. 32:17). When God created the universe, He did so by merely flexing His mighty right arm. With such power at His disposal, nothing is hard for God.

GOD IS ALL-SUSTAINING

After having created the universe, God upholds all that He has made without lifting a finger. The prophet Isaiah calls: "Lift up your eyes on high and see who has created these stars, the One who leads forth their host by number, He calls them all by name; because of the greatness of His might and the strength of His power, not one of them is missing" (Isa. 40:26). God did not create the heavens and the earth only to become a helpless, passive spectator of what He made. To the contrary, God upholds the entire created order moment by moment by His all-sustaining power.

The psalmist urges us to extol God for His might: "Let them praise the name of the LORD, for He commanded and they were created. He has also established them forever and ever; He has made a decree which will not pass away" (Ps. 148:5–6). By His limitless power, God preserves all that He made. He even governs the vast weather patterns. Elihu said, "For to the snow He says, 'Fall on the earth,' and to the downpour and the rain, 'Be strong.' . . . From the breath of God ice is made, and the expanse of the waters is frozen. Also with moisture He loads the thick cloud; He disperses the cloud of His lightning. It changes direction, turning around by His guidance, that it may do whatever He commands it on the face of the inhabited earth" (Job 37:6, 10–12). According to this, God mightily commands every element, from the tiniest ice crystal to the hugest storm.

In the New Testament, we read that God the Father committed to His Son, Jesus Christ, the sustaining of creation. Referring to Christ, Paul writes, "In Him all things hold together" (Col. 1:17). Christ causes all He created to be continually sustained— down to the most minute molecule. The author of Hebrews writes that Jesus Christ "upholds all things by the word of His power" (Heb. 1:3). The universe is constantly being maintained by His great omnipotence. Christ keeps the earth on its axis and sustains its rotation in its orbit around the sun. He upholds all the laws of gravity and thermodynamics, which requires strength of an unimaginable magnitude.

GOD IS ALL-CONTROLLING

God exercises His omnipotence by controlling the affairs of providence. He directs the flow of human history to its appointed end. Ezra records, "The LORD stirred up the spirit of Cyrus king of Persia, so that he sent a proclamation throughout all his kingdom" (Ezra 1:1). God did this so that the Persian king would fulfill His purposes. Even unbelievers yield to the controlling power of God. He powerfully channels the hearts of kings as it pleases Him. He causes the decisions of kings to follow the direction He has foreordained.

By His all-controlling power, God raises up world rulers and places them on their thrones. He lowers other kings by His omnipotence. Daniel says, "It is He who changes the times and the epochs; He removes kings and establishes kings" (Dan. 2:21). God controls not only who are the "kings," but the "times" in which they rule. Nebuchadnezzar was told, "The Most High is ruler over the realm of mankind and bestows it on whomever He wishes" (Dan. 4:32). This mightiest ruler of his day heard this testimony and came to recognize that he was enthroned only because it pleased God for it to be so.

Jesus says to Pilate, "You would have no authority over Me, unless it had been given you from above" (John 19:11). The mightiest rulers on the earth, even those who are unbelievers, are put in a place of authority by God. The apostle John records that God puts into kings what they are to do: "For God has put it in their hearts to execute His purpose by having a common purpose, and by giving their kingdom to the beast, until the words of God will be fulfilled" (Rev. 17:17). The invisible hand of God moves all things forward by His mighty arm of infinite power.

GOD IS ALL-VICTORIOUS

The omnipotence of God causes Him to be always triumphant in the face of any opposition. As the Almighty, He is unhindered by any enemy He faces. After God drowned Pharaoh's hordes, Moses sang: "The LORD is a warrior; the LORD is His name. Pharaoh's chariots and his army He has cast into the sea; and the choicest of his officers are drowned in the Red Sea. . . . Your right hand, O LORD, is majestic in power, Your right hand, O LORD, shatters the enemy" (Ex. 15:3–4, 6). In the parting of the Red Sea, God devastated Pharaoh's mightiest leaders and army with awe-inspiring might.

The psalmist writes: "Why are the nations in an uproar and the peoples devising a vain thing? The kings of the earth take their stand and the rulers take counsel together against the LORD and against His Anointed, saying, 'Let us tear their fetters apart and cast away their cords from us!' He who sits in the heavens laughs, the Lord scoffs at them" (Ps. 2:1–4). God ridicules the insanity of the world's attempt to resist Him. Any opposition mounted against Him will end in certain defeat.

The psalmist testifies, "His right hand and His holy arm have gained the victory for Him" (Ps. 98:1). Whenever God fights with His unrivaled omnipotence, it always results in His victory. Solomon concurs: "The horse is prepared for the day of battle, but victory belongs to the LORD" (Prov. 21:31). Though man prepares his weapons of war, the final outcome belongs to God and whatever His power dictates. There is no human or hellish force that can ever overthrow God. He is immovable, unconquerable, and undefeated.

God is infinitely greater than all the mounted forces of darkness. The devil and his demons are no match for the strength of God. The apostle John declares, "Greater is He who is in you than he who is in the world" (1 John 4:4). The One who indwells believers is immeasurably greater than the ruler of this age. No creature can defeat the efforts of Almighty God. Even if the entire world rose up against God, it would be an unsuccessful revolt.

GOD IS ALL-SAVING

This omnipotent God is also mighty to save sinners from His wrath. In the conversion of His elect, He is able to overcome their natural resistance to the gospel and bring them to faith in Christ. Concerning salvation, Jesus said, "With people this is impossible, but with God all things are possible" (Matt. 19:26). Entrance into the kingdom of God is unattainable for any individual apart from the might of God. But what is unachievable to man is undeniably possible for God. No one lives beyond the saving power of

God. The Almighty can break open the hardest heart and rescue the chief of sinners (1 Tim. 1:15). Divine omnipotence can cause spiritually blind eyes to see the truth (John 9:11, 39) and spiritually deaf ears to hear the effectual call (John 5:25; 10:3, 27).

By His overruling power, God is able to execute His eternal will to save His elect. Paul writes: "Now to Him who is able to do far more abundantly beyond all that we ask or think, according to the power that works within us, to Him be the glory in the church and in Christ Jesus to all generations forever and ever. Amen" (Eph. 3:20–21). The phrase "is able" (Greek *dynamai*) means "to have power, to be strong, to be able to do something." According to these verses, God is more than able to dynamically raise those who are dead in their trespasses to new life in Christ (Eph. 2:1, 5). He can subdue the most stiff-necked person and bring him to faith. He is mighty to guard every believer and fulfill every prophecy. He is able to do far beyond anything we can possibly imagine.

GOD IS ALL-OVERCOMING

Because God is omnipotent, He is therefore able to overcome any opposition that would be brought against Him. None of his eternal purposes can be successfully halted by temporal powers. Job asks: "Were He to snatch away, who could restrain Him? Who could say to Him, 'What are You doing?'" (Job 9:12). The anticipated reply is no one can resist the omnipotent hand of God. Job further declared, "There is no deliverance from Your hand" (Job 10:7). No matter how hard one may try, no one can escape the powerful hand of God. Neither can any person restrain Him. "If He passes by or shuts up, or calls an assembly, who can restrain

Him?" (Job 11:10). The answer to this question is clear. No one can hold back the mighty hand of God.

Job concludes, "I know that You can do all things, and that no purpose of Yours can be thwarted" (Job 42:2). This says God is absolutely irresistible in the exercise of His might. Isaiah confesses the same: "For the LORD of hosts has planned, and who can frustrate it? And as for His stretched-out hand, who can turn it back?" (Isa. 14:27). These rhetorical questions require a negative answer. No individual or earthly force can hinder the advancement of God's sovereign purposes. No one can prevent Him from fulfilling every aspect of His eternal will.

God declares His unstoppable power: "Even from eternity I am He, and there is none who can deliver out of My hand; I act and who can reverse it?" (Isa. 43:13). Again, this rhetorical question anticipates a negative response. The power of God moves forward His providence in history with unstoppable success. Nebuchadnezzar learned this truth, confessing: "All the inhabitants of the earth are accounted as nothing, but He does according to His will in the host of heaven and among the inhabitants of earth; and no one can ward off His hand or say to Him, 'What have You done?'" (Dan. 4:35). No one can mount any effective resistance against Almighty God.

GOD IS ALL-STRENGTHENING

The limitless omnipotence of God is at work within every believer, imparting strength to live the Christian life. Jesus says, "Apart from Me you can do nothing" (John 15:5). Before He departed this world, He explained to His disciples, "I am sending forth the promise of My Father upon you; but you are to stay in the city until you are clothed with power from on high" (Luke 24:49). This cryptic promise foretold the sending of the power of the Holy Spirit, who would enable them to be His witnesses in a hostile world. Jesus announces, "But you will receive power when the Holy Spirit has come upon you; and you shall be My witnesses both in Jerusalem, and in all Judea and Samaria, and even to the remotest part of the earth" (Acts 1:8). In this Great Commission, Jesus promises to endue His people with the abundant power to reach the world with the gospel.

When Paul was inflicted with a thorn in the flesh, God comforted him, "My grace is sufficient for you, for power is perfected in weakness" (2 Cor. 12:9). To which, he responded, "Most gladly, therefore, I will rather boast about my weaknesses, so that the power of Christ may dwell in me." God supplies His people with sufficient—and even abundant—power to fulfill His will. Paul prays for believers "that He would grant you, according to the riches of His glory, to be strengthened with power through His Spirit in the inner man" (Eph. 3:16). He prays that the believers would be "strengthened with all power, according to His glorious might, for the attaining of all steadfastness and patience" (Col. 1:11). Paul reminds Timothy, "For God has not given us a spirit of timidity, but of power and love and discipline" (2 Tim. 1:7). The indwelling Holy Spirit gives the power necessary for believers to glorify God in their words and deeds.

ALL-SUFFICIENT POWER

This divine power is available to every believer as we each press forward in our Christian lives. We can do everything God puts before us by the strength He provides. The apostle Paul confidently says, "I can do all things through Him who strengthens me" (Phil. 4:13). We must rely on the power of God as we fulfill what He has called us to do. When we are the weakest, the power of God is most fully realized in our lives. As we look to Him for strength, He supersedes our frailties with His power.

The supernatural power of the Word of God, when appropriated by faith into our lives, energizes us to do His work. Moreover, the indwelling presence of the Holy Spirit within us gives us the strength we need to fulfill His will. Whatever obstacles we may face in our lives, we are divinely empowered to be more than conquerors in Christ Jesus through this great power. Out of His abundance, God will provide the all-sufficient power for you to follow Him in whatever He has called you to do.

Chapter Twelve

BRILLIANTLY WISE

The Wisdom of God

God's wisdom is seen in the selection of proper ends and of proper means for the accomplishment of those ends.

—Charles Hodge

In the last three chapters, we examined three essential divine attributes—omnipresence, omniscience, and omnipotence. These divine *omni* characteristics form a strong triad of perfections that describe God as being uniquely like no one else. It is one thing for God to possess all knowledge and power, as we have been noting. But He must also possess infinite wisdom to use His knowledge and power for the greatest good. We need to be assured that God is all-wise in the use of His other attributes.

The knowledge of God and His wisdom are not interchangeable terms. Divine knowledge deals with God's possession of all facts about everyone and everything. The wisdom of God deals with the best use of that knowledge for the highest goal. Omniscience is cognitive. Divine wisdom is practical. Wisdom is necessary for God to accomplish all things for His glory and our good. Divine wisdom directs Him to use His exhaustive knowledge and irresistible power to achieve the best outcome in every situation. His good judgment enables Him to use His omnipotence to accomplish the highest good.

If we are to trust God, we need to know that His choices are made with perfect prudence. Divine wisdom leads Him to make the best decisions to reach the highest good. It always moves Him to take the best path in order to reach the best possible destination.

GOD IS ALL-WISE

The whole Bible testifies to this divine attribute of God's wisdom. He alone exercises perfect prudence as He presides over the affairs of providence involving every human life. Job confesses God is "wise in heart" (Job 9:4). Job further announces, "With Him are wisdom and might; to Him belong counsel and understanding" (Job 12:13). The psalmist declares, "O LORD, how many are Your works! In wisdom You have made them all" (Ps. 104:24). Solomon affirms the same: "For the LORD gives wisdom; from His mouth come knowledge and understanding (Prov. 2:6). Again, he states, "There is no wisdom and no understanding and no counsel against the LORD" (Prov. 21:30).

The apostle Paul exclaims, "Oh, the depth of the riches . . . of the wisdom . . . of God!" (Rom. 11:33). He teaches that God is "the only wise God" (Rom. 16:27). Paul speaks of "the manifold wisdom of God" (Eph. 3:10). "Manifold" (Greek *polypoikilos*) means "much variegated, of many different colors," much like Joseph's coat of many colors. The wisdom of God is multidimensional beyond our comprehension. Christ Himself is the One "in whom are hidden all the treasures of wisdom and knowledge" (Col. 2:3).

What are the different aspects of the wisdom of God? The following headings will help us think carefully about this divine attribute.

GOD IS DISCERNING

God possesses penetrating understanding into every life and situation as He administers all the affairs of providence. He perceives every situation for what it truly is. He never misreads any individual or circumstance. Job asks, "But where can wisdom be found? And where is the place of understanding?" (Job 28:12). He answers, "Behold, the fear of the Lord, that is wisdom; and to depart from evil is understanding" (v. 28). In both these verses, divine understanding (Hebrew *binah*) is inseparably connected to wisdom (Hebrew *hokmah*). Wisdom involves understanding that rightly perceives the facts and discerns the right response to what is true.

The psalmist says God is "He who fashions the hearts of them all, He who understands all their works" (Ps. 33:15). God not only knows, but understands the deep, complex workings of the human heart. Solomon added, "To know wisdom and instruction, to discern the sayings of understanding" (Prov. 1:2). The word "discern" (Hebrew *bin*) means "to perceive, understand, to have insight." Discernment with piercing insight is a critical part of divine wisdom. Solomon again states, "The beginning of wisdom is: Acquire wisdom; and with all your acquiring, get understanding" (Prov. 4:7). In this verse, wisdom and understanding are once again inseparably intertwined.

Divine understanding means that God rightly assesses people and situations based upon His perfect knowledge. The Scripture prophesied concerning Jesus Christ, "The Spirit of the LORD will rest on Him, the spirit of wisdom and understanding, the spirit of counsel and strength, the spirit of knowledge and the fear of the LORD" (Isa. 11:2). Because of this discerning wisdom with understanding, "He will not judge by what His eyes see, nor make a decision by what His ears hear" (v. 3). In other words, Jesus will not judge by mere outward appearances, as men do. That kind of judgment would be superficial and deceiving. Instead, He will wisely decide based on His penetrating insight and divine understanding. He will see through the outward facade and peer into the depths of each situation.

GOD IS STRATEGIC

Not only does God perceive circumstances for what they truly are, but He also is strategic in making the best choice from the various options before Him. He exercises good judgment in selecting the best means to reach the greatest good, which is His own glory. The magnification of His own name is the highest end at which He always aims. Wisdom chooses the best path to arrive at that most desired destination. Put another way, wisdom chooses the best means to realize the highest end. Wisdom always deals with both the means and the end.

The highest end of divine wisdom is that the greatest glory be brought to God. The master pursuit of wisdom is the supreme exaltation of God's greatness. Wisdom is always promoting this highest outcome. Paul writes, "Whether, then, you eat or drink or whatever you do, do all to the glory of God" (1 Cor. 10:31). The overarching aim of wisdom is the magnification of divine glory. Paul exults that all things are "to the praise of the glory of His grace" (Eph. 1:6) "in all wisdom and insight" (v. 8).

GOD IS SKILLFUL

Another essential element of divine wisdom is the skill used by God to make the best choice in every situation. The Hebrew word for wisdom (*hokmah*) refers to the practical skill of a master craftsman or gifted artist to make something beautiful with their hands. *Hokmah* was used to describe the skillful embroidering (Ex. 28:3) and metalworking (Ex. 31:3, 6) employed in the tabernacle. The word was also used to describe brilliant military strategy (Isa. 10:13) and polished diplomacy (Deut. 34:9; 2 Sam. 14:20; Ezek. 28:4–5). When applied to God, wisdom refers to the unmatched skill with which He created the universe and the way He oversees the affairs of human history. God uses brilliant discretion in designing creation and administering the affairs of His providence.

In particular, God's skill is profoundly put on display in the creation of the human body and the amazing way it functions. With a sense of awe, David writes, "My frame was not hidden from You, when I was made in secret, and skillfully wrought in the depths of the earth" (Ps. 139:15). Being made "in secret" in "the depths of the earth" is poetic language for his mother's womb, unseen by human eyes. It was there that God superbly wove together his bones and body parts like a multicolored piece of cloth or fine needlepoint. All these threads represent his veins, arteries, muscles, and tendons. "Skillfully wrought" (Hebrew *raqam*) means "to mix colors, to be intricately woven."

With deft design, God tilted the earth at precisely the exact angle and set it in motion at the right speed and the right distance in its orbit around the sun. If the globe were any closer to the sun, human life would burn to a crisp. If this planet were any farther away, all life would be frozen—incapable of survival. God has even counterbalanced the heights of the mountains with the depths of the ocean. The beauty of the earth's terrain testifies to the carefully designed, divine wisdom that shaped it. The cycle of weather patterns and the structure of the animal kingdom also reflect the stunning brilliance of God. Only God in His wondrous wisdom could have crafted the universe to function as efficiently as it does.

GOD IS ASTUTE

In exercising divine wisdom, God always rightly calculates every situation to select the best path to take. He never acts ill-advisedly or overreacts. The wisdom of God is seen in His brilliant management of the affairs of providence. He is always working to cause all things, whether good or evil, to "work together for good" (Rom. 8:28). The trials of life do not occur haphazardly. According to His inscrutable wisdom, God uses even the most disastrous adversity for a greater good—to draw us closer to Him and to conform us into the image of Christ. God even profoundly uses Satan, demons, and worldly evil to bring about His greatest good.

One vivid example is the Genesis narrative of Joseph, who was cruelly sold by his brothers into slavery and forcibly taken to Egypt. When Joseph worked in Potiphar's employment, Potiphar's wife made inappropriate advances toward him, which he resisted. He rightly fled the temptation, but as a result, he suffered unjustly.

He was thrown into prison, from which he was eventually released and, amazingly, was promoted to be second-in-command over Egypt. Looking back on his trials, he realized the hand of an all-wise God was at work. To his betraying brothers, he responded, "You meant evil against me, but God meant it for good" (Gen. 50:20). Only divine wisdom can work for good in such seemingly chaotic circumstances.

During the trials of Job, this suffering saint became worn down and charged God with the mismanagement of his life. At the end of Job's wrestling, God appeared to Job and confronted him over his arrogance: "Where were you when I laid the foundation of the earth?" (Job 38:4). God proceeded to ask Job a series of rapid-fire questions about how the created order functions. In response, Job had no explanation for how the earth and the animal kingdom work so proficiently. He was unable to answer even one of these questions raised by God. How, then, could Job know what God was brilliantly working in his painful difficulties? Job had to trust that God was managing his life through this ordeal with the most astute precision.

GOD IS CONTRARY

Divine wisdom often works in ways that seem entirely counterintuitive to the natural mind of man. God delights in using what the world perceives to be foolish to accomplish His eternal purposes. In redemptive history past, God used the foolishness of the cross to confound the wisdom of this world (1 Cor. 1:18–25). He used the perceived weakness of the death of Christ to overcome what the world considers powerful. In God's master design, the cold-blooded, premeditated murder of the Lord Jesus Christ Himself was at the heart of His eternal purpose. This vile, despicable act was the greatest evil that has ever occurred. Yet Jesus was crucified "by the predetermined plan and foreknowledge of God" (Acts 2:23). This world rose up in an evil conspiracy against the Son of God, calling for His crucifixion, and nailed Him to a cross. It was a blasphemous murder, yet it was the all-wise counsel of God that planned it—accomplishing salvation through this horrific act of violence.

Further, God used the persecution of the early church to spread the gospel far and wide. God used the arrests of Peter and John so that the name of Jesus would be preached to the Sanhedrin (Acts 4:5–22; 5:17–42). He used the gruesome martyrdom of Stephen (Acts 7:54–60) so that Saul of Tarsus would be dramatically converted (Acts 9:3–8). He used the imprisonment of Paul and Silas to plant a vibrant church in Philippi (Acts 16:22–40). In perfect wisdom, God uses the most unusual means, often inscrutable to the human mind, to achieve the highest end. He uses evil, adversity, and trials to bring about the greatest good in the lives of His people.

GOD IS MYSTERIOUS

In the wisdom of God, He has chosen to withhold many divine mysteries from mankind. He has wisely chosen not to make known everything that He is doing in the world. Moses records, "The secret things belong to the LORD our God, but the things revealed belong to us" (Deut. 29:29). In this context, the matters God has "revealed" primarily refer to the divine law He made known through Moses. But what remains a "secret" is how He will carry out His sovereign will. There are many unknown elements of what God is doing in the world. In this sense, there remains the mystery of His providence.

For example, God never revealed to Job the invisible warfare that was taking place between Satan and Him in the unseen world of heaven. God chose to keep this spiritual conflict a mystery, hidden from the understanding of Job. Though a crucial part of this excruciating ordeal, this concealment caused Job to trust God while losing his possessions, children, and health without this knowledge. He stood fast without ever knowing about the challenge issued to the devil by God concerning whether Job would worship Him for nothing. In perfect wisdom, God works in mysterious ways with all His children amid their tribulations. All we can do is trust the perfect wisdom and love of God for His people—that He will reveal what we need to know to persevere in difficulty.

Further, God hides His wisdom from the wise and intelligent of this world. Jesus said, "I praise You, Father, Lord of heaven and earth, that You have hidden these things from the wise and intelligent and have revealed them to infants" (Matt. 11:25). God concealed the truth of the gospel from the self-righteous religious leaders of Israel who appealed to human reason, rather than divine revelation, to make them right before God. He hid it from their eyes, because "God is opposed to the proud, but gives grace to the humble" (James 4:6). The arrogant self-righteous must humble themselves and come to God like small and needy children. They must come to God by submissive faith, trusting explicitly in the gospel of grace and not their own knowledge.

GOD IS UNFATHOMABLE

The wisdom of God far exceeds human comprehension. David testifies: "He has not dealt with us according to our sins, nor rewarded us according to our iniquities. For as high as the heavens are above the earth, so great is His lovingkindness toward those who fear

Him" (Ps. 103:10–11). This is to say, His grace is far beyond our ability to grasp. The boundless mercy of God to forgive sins is far beyond human understanding. God says, "'For My thoughts are not your thoughts, nor are your ways My ways,' declares the LORD. 'For as the heavens are higher than the earth, so are My ways higher than your ways and My thoughts than your thoughts'" (Isa. 55:8–9). We can never fully understand the wisdom of God except those select aspects that He has revealed to us. Paul exclaims, "Oh, the depth of the riches both of the wisdom and knowledge of God!" (Rom. 11:33). Divine wisdom teaches a bottomless ocean of saving mercy so deep that we can never discern its depths.

Divine wisdom in the gospel is inconceivable to man's finite intellect. Paul explains:

> Yet we do speak wisdom among those who are mature; a wisdom, however, not of this age nor of the rulers of this age, who are passing away; but we speak God's wisdom in a mystery, the hidden wisdom which God predestined before the ages to our glory; the wisdom which none of the rulers of this age has understood; for if they had understood it they would not have crucified the Lord of glory; but just as it is written,
>
> "Things which eye has not seen and ear has not heard,
> And which have not entered the heart of man,
> All that God has prepared for those who love Him."
> (1 Cor. 2:6–9)

No human mind would have ever conceived this way of finding acceptance with God. This mystery refers to the plan of salvation in the cross.

The fathomless depth of God's wisdom is best seen in the cross. The infinite genius of God designed the plan of salvation that would require the death of His own Son. The world's best and brightest minds could have never envisioned the spectacular brilliance of this mission. God the Father ordained that His Son would be born of a virgin, to become a man, yet without sin. By His perfect obedience, Jesus fulfilled all the law to secure righteousness for the unrighteous. *Who* but ingenious God could have designed this?

By divine wisdom, Jesus Christ was sentenced to die upon the cross. Paul teaches, "He made Him who knew no sin to be sin on our behalf" (2 Cor. 5:21). All the sins of those who would believe on Christ were transferred to Him. He bore their sins in His body on that tree (1 Peter 2:24). On the cross, He became a curse for those who were cursed under the law (Gal. 3:13). In His death, He became the Lamb of God who took away the sins of the world (John 1:29). Jesus cried out, "It is finished!" (John 19:30), which meant that the sin debt was paid in full on behalf of His people. He was taken down from that cross and placed in a borrowed tomb. On the third day, God raised Him from the dead. *Who* but God could have designed this?

Jesus then ascended back to heaven, where He was enthroned at the right hand of God the Father. All authority in heaven and earth has been given unto Him (Matt. 28:18). "Whoever will call on the name of the Lord will be saved" (Rom. 10:13). By this plan of salvation, God could be both the just and the Justifier (Rom. 3:26). *Who* but God could have designed this? No man could have ever masterminded this plan of salvation. This is the wisdom of God, that He has provided an innocent Substitute to die in our place on Calvary's cross to secure our redemption. Here is "the power of God and the wisdom of God" (1 Cor. 1:24) on full and magnificent display.

WISDOM FOR EVERY PATH

We can trust a God who is all-wise, can we not? He never misdirects us onto the wrong path. He never gives us the wrong counsel when we are at a loss to know what to do. He never has to consult a third party to formulate the best plan for our lives. God always knows what is the best course for us to take. He *always* chooses the right path for us to pursue.

When we are perplexed about which way to turn, James tells us, "If any of you lacks wisdom, let him ask of God, who gives to all generously and without reproach, and it will be given to him" (James 1:5). God possesses all wisdom and imparts it to us when we ask Him in prayer. However, we must ask for His wisdom in faith: "But he must ask in faith without any doubting, for the one who doubts is like the surf of the sea, driven and tossed by the wind" (v. 6). We must pray with confident trust, without any lack of faith that God's way is the best path for us to take.

God desires to lead us by His wisdom. He has already charted the course we should take. We must look to Him and follow the path so clearly marked in His Word. This divinely marked-out way will surely lead to our holiness and happiness—and the highest end of all, the glory of God exalted.

Chapter Thirteen

ABSOLUTELY TRUE

The Truthfulness of God

*Opinions alter, but truth certified by God can
no more change than the God who uttered them.*

—CHARLES H. SPURGEON

Whenever we study the attributes of God, there are inevitable questions that arise in our minds. One such important question raised is: How reliable is the self-revelation that God has made known to us? Does God give us a trustworthy self-disclosure of Himself? How accurate is what God says about any matter? The answers to this series of questions are vitally important to our faith.

Lest there be any misunderstanding, the Bible teaches that God *is* truth. In no uncertain terms, it declares that He speaks only that which reveals what something truly is. Accordingly, there is no greater truth than what God speaks about Himself. We may be assured that whatever God says about Himself is absolutely true. He alone knows Himself. Whatever He says is who He really is.

This being so, another question needs to be raised: What is the nature of truth? In a word, truth means *reality*. It is the way anything truly is. Truth is not how things may appear to be. It is not what the majority of people conjecture truth to be. It is not even what we may want something to be. Truth is whatever God says is reality. Truth is whatever conforms to the mind and character of God.

Truth is made known by God in specific words in the Scripture that are clearly defined and have a precise meaning. In the Bible, God communicates cognitive truth with objective words that yield an exact meaning. The truth is never vague or indefinite. God does not speak in ambiguous terms. He does not speak with generalities that cannot be assigned a clear-cut meaning. Truth is never uncertain or unclear. To the contrary, truth is precise, explicit, exact, and crystal clear. It is factual, rational, and objective.

The written Word of God is not to be subjectively understood by the personal whims of the individual. It does not mean one thing to one person and something else to another person. Rather, the truth has been made known with black-and-white words that can be parsed and accurately defined. It is expressed in actual words that can be studied and interpreted. It is to be rationally understood. Whatever God says is absolutely true, whether it coincides with a person's preconceived notions or not.

What are the various aspects of the truthfulness with which God speaks? How are we to understand the nature of the veracity of His Word? The following headings will help us think through this important subject about who God is.

GOD IS TRUTH

Starting at the most basic level, the Bible asserts that the very nature of God is truth itself. David writes that He is the "God of truth" (Ps. 31:5). Likewise, Isaiah records, He is "the God of truth" (Isa. 65:16). This is to say, God is truth, and all truth comes from Him. It does not originate from this fallen world. It does not arise out of the twisted culture around us. Nor does it come from man's self-conceived opinions. Truth is not found necessarily in the traditions of men. It does not proceed from within a person. Instead, truth comes down from above. It comes exclusively from the mind of God Himself. He is the Author of all truth, its sole Source and Revealer. God is the Judge and Arbitrator of all truth. Truth is whatever God says anything is.

Being coequal with God the Father, Jesus Christ also claims to speak the truth. He plainly says, "I am . . . the truth" (John 14:6). By this emphatic claim, Jesus asserts that He possesses an exclusive monopoly on the truth. The definite article *the* before "truth" means He is the *only* truth. He states there is no truth outside Himself. He is not merely one of many voices contributing to the collective body of truth. To the contrary, the apostle Paul dogmatically affirms that "truth is in Jesus" (Eph. 4:21). That is, all truth is found solely in Him. Further, Jesus is "the Amen, the faithful and true Witness" (Rev. 3:14). In other words, He alone testifies to the true reality of all things.

God the Holy Spirit is also identified as "the Spirit of truth" (John 14:17; 15:26; 16:13). By His work in the inspiration of Scripture (Heb. 3:7), the Spirit breathed out "the word of truth" (2 Tim. 2:15). To understand the truth, every person must be personally taught by the Holy Spirit Himself. Though God has given gifted leaders to the church to provide instruction in the truth (Eph. 4:11), they are, at best, fallible teachers. There is only one infallible, primary Teacher, the Holy Spirit, who is the internal Teacher of truth. As the Spirit reveals the truth, He is entirely trustworthy in whatever enlightenment He gives.

GOD IS PRECISE

Whatever God says is inerrant because He Himself is holy. Thus, He is incapable of making any error. A perfect God can speak only perfect words. Whatever God says flows from His own flawless nature. Whatever He speaks is free from falsehoods. This extends down to the most minute detail of whatever He addresses. Concerning Himself, God never inaccurately misrepresents who He is. He never makes a mistake in what He reveals about His own being or the world He has created.

The psalmist writes, "The sum of Your word is truth" (Ps. 119:160). In other words, "the sum"—meaning the whole of divine revelation in the written Word—is undefiled, unvarnished, and unadulterated truth.

In everything God speaks, He states what is true, down to the smallest detail. Jesus says, "For truly I say to you, until heaven and earth pass away, not the smallest letter or stroke shall pass from the Law until all is accomplished" (Matt. 5:18). Here, Jesus affirms the exact precision with which God speaks. The Scripture is accurate down to the smallest stroke and letter.

Jesus confirms the same when He prayed to the Father, "Your word is truth" (John 17:17). The Lord is saying that holy God can only say what is truth and without error. Paul writes, "Let

God be found true, though every man be found a liar" (Rom. 3:4). This affirms that whatever God speaks is true, whether it pertains to matters of faith and practice, or science and geography. Every historical event recorded in the Bible is a trustworthy account, no matter how miraculous or extraordinary the event was. Every doctrine taught by God is trustworthy, because He Himself *is* truth.

GOD IS INFALLIBLE

As God speaks, He reveals what is infallibly true. This distinction means that whatever He says will surely come to pass. Balaam says: "God is not a man, that He should lie, nor a son of man, that He should repent; has He said, and will He not do it? Or has He spoken, and will He not make it good?" (Num. 23:19). Whatever God announces will certainly be fulfilled. Whatever promise He makes will undoubtedly be kept. Whatever prophecy He utters will assuredly be realized. Every judgment He renders will necessarily be executed.

The infallibility of the written Word of God means He is faithful to keep all He promises. He will accomplish whatever He pledges to do. The psalmist writes, "All Your commandments are faithful" (Ps. 119:86). "Faithful" (Hebrew *emunah*) means "firmness, steadfastness, steadiness." The psalmist writes, "Your faithfulness continues throughout all generations; You established the earth, and it stands" (v. 90). Here, the Word of God is identified by this brief but meaningful title, "faithfulness." This means God is forever committed to keeping the promises He has made to His people through all generations. As God established the earth by His spoken word and it stood fast, He speaks in His written

Word, and it will come to pass. The psalmist elaborates, "You have commanded Your testimonies in righteousness and exceeding faithfulness" (v. 138). Whatever God says, He will faithfully bring it to pass.

Accordingly, Isaiah records, "The grass withers, the flower fades, but the word of our God stands forever" (Isa. 40:8). This statement affirms that whatever God says, He will cause it to be fulfilled into eternity future. God Himself announces, "For as the rain and the snow come down from heaven, and do not return there without watering the earth and making it bear and sprout, and furnishing seed to the sower and bread to the eater; so will My word be which goes forth from My mouth; it will not return to Me empty, without accomplishing what I desire, and without succeeding in the matter for which I sent it" (Isa. 55:10–11). The rain that comes down from the skies accomplishes its divinely intended purpose. It meets physical needs by supplying water to drink and refreshing the crops to grow abundantly. In the same way, the Word of God comes down from heaven and fulfills what He intends in spiritual lives. The infallible truth of God saves and sanctifies those for whom it is intended.

Though men make promises but rarely keep them, God never will abandon His word. Jesus Christ, the Son of God, is "the faithful witness" (Rev. 1:5), meaning He is always faithful to the truth. At His second coming, Jesus is depicted as descending from heaven as the One who is "Faithful and True" (Rev. 19:11). That is, He is the embodiment of truth. Whatever He speaks conforms perfectly with reality. The written truth in Scripture is an entirely trustworthy record, to the end of the age.

GOD IS OUTSPOKEN

Whatever God says, He does so in a bold, outspoken manner. He has no hesitation in giving a full disclosure of the truth on any subject. When He speaks, He holds back no necessary information. In whatever He addresses, God is direct and straightforward. He makes no attempt to soften His hard sayings. He never reshapes His truth to make it palatable to carnal ears. He never sugarcoats His message. God always tells it like it is, never backing away from complex issues. Whatever God speaks is said in the open, always up-front and candid in His pronouncements.

The people in Jesus' day said about Him, "He is speaking publicly" (John 7:26). Christ spoke "publicly" (Greek *parrēsia*), or "boldly" and "confidently." What Jesus said, He announced for all to hear. Nothing was held back or concealed. Jesus said, "The things which I heard from Him, these I speak to the world" (John 8:26). Jesus publicly proclaimed what the Father had revealed to Him in private. He shouted the truth from the rooftops, as it were, with all boldness.

When questioned by the high priest about His teaching, Jesus answered: "I have spoken openly to the world; I always taught in synagogues and in the temple, where all the Jews come together; and I spoke nothing in secret" (John 18:20). Even Caiaphas recognized that Jesus was outspoken in the declaration of the truth, even provocative and controversial. No essential doctrine concerning salvation was hidden by Jesus. He spoke the truth pointedly, regardless of who it may have offended. He did not tickle ears to make reality seem more soothing. He did not pull back from what had to be proclaimed. He was transparent and candid in what He asserted. He made no effort to soft-pedal the truth.

GOD IS CLEAR

Whenever God speaks, He does so in the clearest manner. He never obscures or muddles the truth. David writes, "The commandment of the LORD is pure" (Ps. 19:8). The word translated "pure" (Hebrew *bar*) means it is "clear" and "lucid." The pronouncements of God are not cryptic or enigmatic. God never communicates matters of salvation and sanctification with smoke and mirrors. The Word of God always shines brightly, clearly revealing the truth for all to see. This is a direct claim for the perspicuity of all God says in His Word. The psalmist says, "Your word is a lamp to my feet and a light to my path" (Ps. 119:105). In other words, truth is not cloudy or murky. Instead, it shines like a bright lamp in overwhelming darkness. Any problems in understanding what God says are not because He is unclear or hard to understand. Rather, the limitation lies with the finite person, not with God.

Jesus made this very point with the religious leaders of Israel. He posed to them this question: "Have you not read that He who created them from the beginning made them male and female?" (Matt. 19:4). This quotation is from Genesis 1:27 and is followed by another citation from Genesis 2:24. The implication Jesus was making was this: If they could read the Scripture, they would clearly understand what God means in His written Word. On another occasion, Jesus addressed the Pharisees and raised the same question: "Have you not read what David did when he became hungry, he and his companions?" (Matt. 12:3). If they could simply read, they would know the truth God has spoken.

Once more, Jesus said to the Sadducees, "But regarding the resurrection of the dead, have you not read what was spoken to you by God?" (Matt. 22:31). Jesus expected them to understand what God has stated plainly. His Word is abundantly clear in revealing what He teaches. It is out in the open for all to read and know the purpose of God.

GOD IS COMMANDING

Moreover, whatever God says in His Word is authoritative. His pronouncements command the obedience of every human heart. His words place demands on mankind. The psalmist says, "Then I shall not be ashamed when I look upon all Your commandments" (Ps. 119:6). This verse states that the Bible contains the "commandments" of God. This is to say, these are not His suggestions. Neither are they His opinions or preferences. What God says in the Scripture is never meant to be merely intriguing to the reader. Nor is it meant to satisfy the vain curiosity of people—it is meant to be heeded.

Divine truth is never issued with a "take or leave it" caveat. It is never intended to be merely one more option among many possibilities vying for our attention. Instead, truth is authoritative, possessing the right to make demands on our lives. It is arresting and demands our full and unwavering allegiance.

Divine truth always calls for our response. Jesus says: "Everyone who comes to Me and hears My words and acts on them, I will show you whom he is like: he is like a man building a house, who dug deep and laid a foundation on the rock; and when a flood occurred, the torrent burst against that house and could not shake it, because it had been well built" (Luke 6:47–48). Jesus emphatically states that His truth mandates decisive obedience. Truth first instructs our minds, but it also challenges our wills. We must respond with obedience to all that He says.

James says, "Prove yourselves doers of the word, and not merely hearers who delude themselves" (James 1:22). In response to the Word of God, our consciences must be bound to the truth. It is, therefore, necessary that we act on what we know to be true.

GOD IS CONSISTENT

In addition, the truthfulness of God means that He speaks in one unified body of truth. In whatever He says, He never contradicts Himself. No statement of God ever negates or cancels out another divine statement. Every divinely spoken truth is consistently woven together to form one seamless tapestry of divine revelation. Every doctrine fits perfectly into place to form "one faith" (Eph. 4:5). The Christian faith is "the faith which was once for all handed down to the saints" (Jude 3). Every doctrine holds together to form one consistent standard of revealed truth. Every divine teaching perfectly meshes together with the others like individual bricks in a towering wall to form one coherent system of theology.

In this sense, truth is singular. No one truth is a disconnected fragment, unrelated to other truths in the Bible. All truth holds together in the mind of God. Every doctrine is interrelated with every other teaching He gives. From Genesis to Revelation, the whole counsel of God fits together perfectly without any contradiction. The first church was taught "the apostles' teaching" (Acts 2:42). In this verse, the definite article "the" indicates they taught one united body of truth that is perfectly interconnected. This network of doctrine is elsewhere known as "the standard of sound words" (2 Tim. 1:13). The truth of God presents one comprehensive, consistent framework of truth.

GOD IS UNALTERABLE

The truth that God speaks is irrevocable and can never be altered or amended. The psalmist testifies, "Forever, O LORD, Your word is settled in heaven" (Ps. 119:89). "Settled" (Hebrew *natsab*) means "to be fixed, to cause to stand erect." The truth that God speaks is fixed and stands forever, from eternity past into eternity future. Throughout the centuries, there will never be any change to the infallible words that God speaks. The psalmist states, "Of old I have known from Your testimonies that You have founded them forever" (v. 152). Whatever God says will never be revoked, but will truly last "forever." Once more, he affirms, "The sum of Your word is truth, and every one of Your righteous ordinances is everlasting" (v. 160). This truth spoken by God will never be invalidated and can never be rescinded.

The prophet Isaiah also maintains the truth of God is irrevocable: "The grass withers, the flower fades, but the word of our God stands forever" (Isa. 40:8). By this, he means the philosophies of this world are withering and perishing, but the truth of God endures throughout time and eternity. Jesus likewise says, "For truly I say to you, until heaven and earth pass away, not the smallest letter or stroke shall pass from the Law until all is accomplished" (Matt. 5:18). This is to say, the created order will one day cease to exist in its present form, but every divine truth in the law will be fulfilled and remain to the end.

Truth transcends all shifting social mores. It rises above the changing cultural norms. No matter where people are on the globe, they need to hear and heed the unalterable truth of God. Jesus said, "Heaven and earth will pass away, but My words will not pass away" (Matt. 24:35). In other words, whatever God says will never be changed. Further, He said, "It is easier for heaven and earth to pass away than for one stroke of a letter of the Law to fail" (Luke 16:17). No teaching of Scripture will ever be abrogated. In the end, every person's standing before God will be determined by his relationship to the forever-standing truth that proceeds from God's mouth. Simply put, no truth of God will ever be annulled.

GOD IS ILLUMINATING

In one way or another, any individual truth spoken by God helps illumine other truths in the Bible. Mere human reasoning by itself is not sufficient to find the truth. God must grant the understanding necessary to comprehend His Word. The psalmist said, "Blessed are You, O LORD; teach me Your statutes" (Ps. 119:12). He recognizes that God must enlighten the mind in order for anyone to learn His truth. Throughout this enormous psalm, the psalmist makes this recurring plea for illumination: "Teach me Your statutes" (v. 26). It is a request reiterated many more times in this psalm (vv. 64, 108, 124, 135, 171). The fact is, God Himself must inwardly teach anyone who would know the truth. The psalmist asks, "Open my eyes, that I may behold wonderful things from Your law" (v. 18). Here, He realizes that God must enlighten his understanding of Scripture if he hopes to grasp its true meaning.

Jesus recognized this need for divine illumination. He said to Peter, "Blessed are you, Simon Barjona, because flesh and blood did not reveal this to you, but My Father who is in heaven" (Matt. 16:17). Jesus acknowledged that God the Father had opened Peter's eyes to perceive the truth concerning who He is. The same is true for everyone who would know the truth. It must be revealed through divine intervention before it can be discovered and embraced.

Jesus says, "But when He, the Spirit of truth, comes, He will guide you into all the truth; for He will not speak on His own initiative, but whatever He hears, He will speak; and He will disclose to you what is to come" (John 16:13). God Himself must teach His own truth to His children—and He delights to do so.

The apostle Paul prays that God would illumine the understanding of divine truth in the minds of believers: "That the God of our Lord Jesus Christ, the Father of glory, may give to you a spirit of wisdom and of revelation in the knowledge of Him. I pray that the eyes of your heart may be enlightened, so that you will know what is the hope of His calling, what are the riches of the glory of His inheritance in the saints" (Eph. 1:17–18). By this intercession, Paul prays for the minds of his readers to be enlightened in the knowledge of the truth.

THE TRUTH SETS YOU FREE

It is the knowledge of the Scripture that each one of us must possess. Apart from the truth, no one can be saved. Neither can anyone be sanctified. Jesus says, "You will know the truth, and the truth will make you free" (John 8:32). The truth alone can liberate us from our bondage to the chains of our sin. To know the written Word of God is indispensable to knowing God.

Are you being confronted with the truth of who God is? You must respond in faith to the gravity of what is being made known to you. Truth always demands a response. It always requires a step of active obedience to what it asserts. To know the truth and not respond to it in humble obedience is to not actually know the truth—at least not in the innermost depths of your being.

The God of truth is calling you to live in compliance with His Word. If you are not a born-again believer, this begins with the first step of faith in His Son, Jesus Christ. If you are a believer, this requires your obedient faith to all that He reveals in His Word. May God give you much faith to step out and trust Him, for He holds the keys to the infinite storehouse of all truth.

Chapter Fourteen

GRACIOUSLY KIND

The Goodness of God

God's goodness is the root of all goodness; and our goodness,
if we have any, springs from His goodness.

—WILLIAM TYNDALE

I n earlier chapters, we considered the sovereignty and omnipotence of God. Given these truths about the divine nature, we might be tempted to conclude that He is a stern dictator, a detached deity, uncaring toward His creation. We might jump to the conclusion that God is a stoic Sovereign, devoid of feelings, merely making calculated chess moves from heaven. Nothing could be further from the truth.

Truthfully, God is the very opposite. The Bible teaches that He is good and gracious, kind and caring. In fact, God is so good that the word *God* in English is derived from the German word that means "good." His heart is a perpetual fountain of goodness, flowing like a swelling river that overruns its banks. We are literally deluged with the kindness of God, immersed with

His benevolence. An ocean of divine benevolence is being lavished upon us from His throne of grace. God is the Source of all good things, and He delights in bestowing good gifts upon His creation.

As we think about His goodness, we gather our thoughts under the following headings.

GOD IS GOOD

Throughout the Scripture, the goodness of God is repeatedly stressed. When Moses asked to see the glory of God, He replied, "I Myself will make all My goodness pass before you" (Ex. 33:19). This indicates that the goodness of God is at the epicenter of His divine glory. David announces, "Surely goodness and lovingkindness will follow me all the days of my life" (Ps. 23:6). He knows he will always be pursued by the Lord's goodness throughout his life. David recounts, "Good and upright is the LORD" (Ps. 25:8). The word "good" (Hebrew *tob*) carries the idea of His abundant kindness and benevolence. His goodness is His charitable disposition to be generous to His creatures. It speaks to the graciousness of God in His dealing mercifully with us.

Again, David pronounces, "How great is Your goodness" (Ps. 31:19). The idea conveyed is that the goodness of God is enormous. David invites his readers, "O taste and see that the LORD is good" (Ps. 34:8). The one who knows God will experience the sweet taste of His goodness. Once more, David exclaims, "For You, Lord, are good" (Ps. 86:5). Spoken in the present tense, this states that God is always good. Elsewhere, the psalmist rejoices as a constant reality, "For the LORD is good" (Ps. 100:5). Again, he says, "Oh give thanks to the LORD, for He is good" (Ps. 106:1).

This repeated testimony flows from the pen of the psalmist—the goodness of God is great in its abundant supply.

The apostle Paul announces "the riches of His kindness" (Rom. 2:4). God is unimaginably wealthy in goodness and delights in lavishing it on the world He created. Even in troubling trials, we must remain convinced that God is good (Gen. 50:20). When we look at our circumstances or observe the fallen world around us, we may be tempted to waver in our settled confidence in the goodness of God. But when we look into the Word of God, the testimony of Scripture repeatedly reaffirms the extreme abundance of His goodness.

GOD IS GENEROUS

The goodness of God is not rationed out in small, miserly doses. Rather, He is most generous to provide for the needs of His people. This was certainly the experience of Israel during their wilderness journey. God provided for their needs throughout this prolonged trip with water in the desert (Ex. 15:22–27). He sent them bread—which they called manna—every morning (Ex. 16:4). Moreover, God gave them meat to eat in the evening (Ex. 16:8). When the people thirsted again, Moses struck the rock, and God supplied them with water to drink (Ex. 17:1–7). God further gave His law to guide them into the fullness of His blessing (Ex. 20–40). All this represents the abundant provision of God toward His people.

God is so good that He even shows kindness to the animal kingdom. He asked Job: "Can you hunt the prey for the lion, or satisfy the appetite of the young lions, when they crouch in their dens and lie in wait in their lair? Who prepares for the raven its nourishment when its young cry to God and wander about without food?" (Job 38:39–41). These rhetorical questions are intended to teach Job that God Himself provides them food. No man is able to crawl up the side of the cliff, where the raven has built a nest in order to feed it. But God feeds the young lions and the ravens with attentive care.

The psalmist David testifies that God provides for His people in their most trying circumstances: "You prepare a table before me in the presence of my enemies; You have anointed my head with oil; my cup overflows" (Ps. 23:5). Here, David represents God as a gracious host who prepares a sumptuous banquet feast for those who enter His kingdom. Even in the midst of threatening enemies, God's provision is lavishly given. His supply is being poured into David's cup until it is overflowing and cannot be contained. Simply put, God's supply far exceeds his needs.

The psalmist further explains the divine goodness to the animal kingdom: "There is the sea, great and broad, in which are swarms without number, animals both small and great. . . . They all wait for You to give them their food in due season. You give to them, they gather it up; You open Your hand, they are satisfied with good" (Ps. 104:25, 27–28). God is generous to feed all His creatures. The psalmist reminds us that He "gives food to all flesh, for His lovingkindness is everlasting" (Ps. 136:25). This generosity is seen toward those who dwell throughout the whole earth. God provides them with sunlight, clean air, fresh water, and sustaining food.

David praises God for His goodness, saying: "The LORD is good to all, and His mercies are over all His works" (Ps. 145:9). The generosity of God is abundant to all peoples everywhere. Another psalmist announces this same truth, that God bountifully feeds

His creatures: "He gives to the beast its food, and to the young ravens which cry" (Ps. 147:9). There are, of course, exceptions to this (Ps. 34:10), but they are not the rule.

Jesus affirms the same: "Look at the birds of the air, that they do not sow, nor reap nor gather into barns, and yet your heavenly Father feeds them" (Matt. 6:26). God showers His benevolence on the birds in the air, the fish in the sea, and the creatures on the earth. Likewise, God cares for those made in His own image: "If God so clothes the grass of the field, which is alive today and tomorrow is thrown into the furnace, will He not much more clothe you?" (v. 30). A continual flow of divine goodness is streaming into the lives of His people by His openhanded providential care.

GOD IS GRACIOUS

God even extends His goodness to unbelievers who live outside His kingdom. His general benevolence toward all people, sometimes known as common grace, is extended to those who are strangers to His saving grace. David confesses, "You open Your hand and satisfy the desire of every living thing" (Ps. 145:16). As unbelievers persist in their sins, God nevertheless extends His hand to give them good gifts. For example, He allows unbelievers to enter into marriage and enjoy having children. God permits them to have an education, gain employment, and advance in their careers. He affords unbelievers the luxury to travel and see the wonders of His creation. He does not withhold His goodness from them but provides it for their enjoyment.

Jesus confirms this when He says God "causes His sun to rise on the evil and the good, and sends rain on the righteous and the unrighteous" (Matt. 5:45). According to these words, the goodness of God is not reserved exclusively for believers. Instead, it is extended to unbelievers as well. The benefits from the sun and weather bear a silent testimony of the goodness of God. Paul said the same to the unbelievers in Athens: God "did good and gave you rains from heaven and fruitful seasons, satisfying your hearts with food and gladness" (Acts 14:17). Not everyone, however, receives the same amount of divine goodness. Some unbelievers are wealthier than others. Some have better health than others or have more education. God dispenses gifts as His wisdom directs Him. Not every person experiences the same measure of gifts, but God is still wholly good.

GOD IS INDISCRIMINATE

In His goodness, God also causes even unbelievers to prosper in their work. There are times when God is so good to unbelievers that this prosperity can cause believers to become envious and stumble into sin. In His mysterious will, God sometimes bestows more temporal blessings on strangers to His kingdom than on its citizens. Asaph confides, "For I was envious of the arrogant as I saw the prosperity of the wicked. For there are no pains in their death, and their body is fat" (Ps. 73:3–4). He noted that many unbelievers eat better than the righteous, and their bodies are bulging with fat. They even seem to die content with a happy countenance. Asaph adds, "They are not in trouble as other men, nor are they plagued like mankind" (v. 5). God is so good to those who are devoid of saving faith that it almost caused Asaph to stumble. From his vantage point, believers seem to suffer greater adversity in life than unbelievers.

It was not until Asaph went into the house of the Lord that he regained the right perspective (v. 17). In the temple, he heard the Word of God taught. Under the sound of the Word, he remembered the end of the wicked. When their fleeting days of enjoying their present prosperity come to an end, they will immediately suffer "destruction" (v. 18). "They are utterly swept away by sudden terrors!" (v. 19). In the flames below, they will suffer dreadful weeping and gnashing of teeth. Only then did Asaph regain the right perspective. Though God lavishes His goodness on unbelievers, Asaph finally saw their end apart from His intervening grace.

GOD IS JUDICIOUS

Beyond His care of unbelievers, God provides for those who put their trust in His saving grace with judicious wisdom. He does not always endow believers with the same physical abundance with which He blesses unbelievers. Neither do all believers receive the same provisions. God gives with inscrutable judgment to His children. With perfect discretion, He pours out earthly blessings on the saints. David testifies, "They who seek the LORD shall not be in want of any good thing" (Ps. 34:10). Believers are the only ones who truly seek the Lord. They will have their needs met by God according to what He deems best.

David acknowledges God's goodness when he writes, "I have been young and now I am old, yet I have not seen the righteous forsaken or his descendants begging bread" (Ps. 37:25). God is good to those who put their trust in Him. The psalmist reassures us: "The LORD God is a sun and shield; the LORD gives grace and glory; no good thing does He withhold from those who walk uprightly" (Ps. 84:11). It pleases God to supply for the needs of His own people.

Jesus affirmed this willingness of God to provide for His children when He said: "Ask, and it will be given to you; seek, and you will find; knock, and it will be opened to you" (Matt. 7:7). This indicates God's desire to meet the needs of His own children. Jesus added, "For everyone who asks receives, and he who seeks finds, and to him who knocks it will be opened" (v. 8). This indicates how willing God is to provide for His sons and daughters. Jesus concluded, "Or what man is there among you who, when his son asks for a loaf, will give him a stone? Or if he asks for a fish, he will not give him a snake, will he? If you then, being evil, know how to give good gifts to your children, how much more will your Father who is in heaven give what is good to those who ask Him!" (vv. 9–11).

Jesus understood that even sinful fathers give their children good gifts. How much more will our heavenly Father give His children what is good? To a far greater extent, God provides good things for those who are born again into His family. Paul writes, "He who did not spare His own Son, but delivered Him over for us all, how will He not also with Him freely give us all things?" (Rom. 8:32). God invites us to present our needs before Him. He desires that we ask Him to provide for us according to His perfect will.

GOD IS PATIENT

The goodness of God is further seen in the patience with which He deals with men and women. God proclaimed to Moses that He is "slow to anger" (Ex. 34:6). With much long-suffering, God gives people time to repent and turn to Him. Moses prayed, acknowledging what God revealed to him, that "the LORD is slow to anger" (Num. 14:18; cf. Ps. 103:8; 145:8). God is patient even with the nonelect, who are passed over by His sovereign grace. Paul writes, "What if God, although willing to demonstrate His wrath and to make His power known, endured with much patience vessels of wrath prepared for destruction?" (Rom. 9:22). God's goodness leads Him to exercise "much patience" toward sinners. He does not immediately consign an unbeliever to hell after his first sin.

This patience of God resulted in the conversion of Saul of Tarsus. Once an avowed opponent of the gospel, the apostle Paul writes: "Yet for this reason I found mercy, so that in me as the foremost, Jesus Christ might demonstrate His perfect patience as an example for those who would believe in Him for eternal life" (1 Tim. 1:16). As in the case of Paul, God's long-suffering provides the elect with the necessary time they need to believe in Jesus Christ. The divinely appointed moment is also the goodness of God.

Never was divine patience more evident than in the pre-flood days of Noah. Peter describes that dark hour "when the patience of God kept waiting in the days of Noah, during the construction of the ark, in which a few, that is, eight persons, were brought safely through the water" (1 Peter 3:20). Though none outside of Noah's family believed, God waited patiently for 120 years for sinners to repent. As Noah built the ark, God remained forbearing with the lost. He gave them extended opportunities to be saved from the cataclysmic flood.

Peter reminded the early believers that the patience of God resulted in their salvation. He announces, "The Lord is not slow about His promise, as some count slowness, but is patient toward you, not wishing for any to perish but for all to come to repentance" (2 Peter 3:9). He writes, "Therefore, beloved, since you look for these things, be diligent to be found by Him in peace, spotless and blameless, and regard the patience of our Lord as salvation" (vv. 14–15). It was this divine patience that allowed their salvation to take place.

GOD IS GUIDING

Another important aspect of the goodness of God is the personal guidance He gives to individuals who put their trust in Him. David writes, "He guides me in the paths of righteousness for His name's sake" (Ps. 23:3). As the Good Shepherd, God directs His people into "green pastures" and beside "quiet waters" (v. 2). God never leads into sin, but always into holiness of life. David also states, "The steps of a man are established by the LORD, and He delights in his way. When he falls, he will not be hurled headlong, because the LORD is the One who holds his hand" (Ps. 37:23–24). God gives individual direction into His will, "which is good and acceptable and perfect" (Rom. 12:2). God always leads His people onto this chosen path of personal holiness.

David was assured that this divine guidance for his life was for the glory of God. He acknowledges, "For Your name's sake You will lead me and guide me" (Ps. 31:3). Through the many dangers and detours of this world, David remained confident that God was leading in his life. He prays for this path to be clearly made known before him: "O LORD, lead me in Your righteousness because of my foes; make Your way straight before me" (Ps. 5:8). God will never lead His people into sin, but only down paths of personal holiness.

This guidance was experienced in the earthly life of Jesus Christ. Being "full of the Holy Spirit," Jesus was "led around by the Spirit in the wilderness" to be tempted by the devil (Luke 4:1–2).

It was this leading by God that was for a far greater purpose. Even so, the Holy Spirit leads believers into personal holiness: "For all who are being led by the Spirit of God, these are sons of God" (Rom. 8:14). This direction is evidence of the goodness of God toward us.

GOD IS GUARDING

The goodness of God is likewise seen in the protection He gives to His people. It was initially seen in the garden of Eden when He placed the first couple in paradise to enjoy the abundance of His goodness. They had the entire world to enjoy. But there was only one tree from which they were forbidden to eat, namely the Tree of Knowledge of Good and Evil (Gen. 2:17). This prohibition was an expression of the goodness of God, as it protected their minds from being polluted with evil. Such knowledge would rob them of their happiness. From this we learn that every divine commandment that prohibits us from doing something is an expression of His goodness. Such a restriction is a protection intended to prevent us from harm.

When Satan slithered onto the scene, he drew attention to this one tree from which Adam and Eve were forbidden to eat. The subtle implication was that God was withholding His blessings from them. The lie was that the Creator was not being good to them. If God were truly good, He would not restrict them from eating from this beautiful tree. Eve bought into that false narrative. But it was the goodness of God that built this wall of protection around this forbidden tree. This warning was an expression of His infinite kindness.

Job enjoyed the protective care of God, who "made a hedge

about him and his house and all that he has, on every side" (Job 1:10). Though Satan tried, he could not penetrate the shield of defense around him. This was an expression of God's goodness toward him. When that hedge was later removed, it likewise, ultimately, was for a greater good.

ALL FOR GOOD

God is always working for the good of His children. Paul writes, "And we know that God causes all things to work together for good to those who love God, to those who are called according to His purpose" (Rom. 8:28). This "good" is defined in what follows as being "conformed to the image of His Son" (v. 29). Because God is good, He is always working for our good—which is the lifelong process of shaping us into Christlikeness. There is no greater good in this world than for us to become like Jesus Christ. This spiritual growth leads to our greater happiness and joy.

God is causing "all things"—both good things and bad things, prosperity and adversity—to be interwoven into one master purpose that He is constantly working in our lives. Nothing is out of His control. Everything is under His guidance. "All things" are working for our good, because God Himself is good.

Chapter Fifteen

MERCIFULLY SAVING

The Grace of God

Grace signifies that favor with which God receives us,
forgiving our sins and justifying us freely through Christ.
—MARTIN LUTHER

The very nature of God is to rescue those who are perishing. Though He is under no obligation to intervene, the heart of God yearns to save those who are in great spiritual peril. He delights to deliver those whose souls are in grave danger of eternal destruction. The extraordinary riches of His grace are most clearly demonstrated in His saving acts, to recapture those who are in danger of suffering under His wrath. This is the unfathomable greatness of the saving grace of God.

Divine grace is God's unmerited favor toward unworthy sinners that delivers them from His just condemnation and bestows on them His forgiveness and righteousness. It is the attribute of God by which He withholds from sinful mankind what they truly deserve—judgment. Instead, He gives them what they do not deserve—salvation. Grace is given freely by God, without any cost, to the one who receives it by faith. It is the extraordinary gift of God that cannot be merited or earned. It is given without cost to those who have utterly no claim on it. Grace is initiated, accomplished, and completed by God alone.

The apostle Paul stresses the freeness of this grace when he writes, "But if it is by grace, it is no longer on the basis of works, otherwise grace is no longer grace" (Rom. 11:6). In matters of eternal salvation, grace and works cannot coexist. They are incapable of working together. They are incompatible—mutually exclusive, never inclusive. The reality is that saving grace is always freely bestowed, never earned. It is never a reward for the righteous, but a gift for the guilty. The apostle Paul writes: "For by grace you have been saved through faith; and that not of yourselves, it is the gift of God; not as a result of works, so that no one may boast" (Eph. 2:8–9). In His lavishing nature, God freely gives His unmerited grace to undeserving sinners. He delights to show mercy to those who are hopelessly devastated by sin.

Several aspects of the grace of God require our attention in this chapter.

GOD IS MERCIFUL

The saving grace of God is thrust into action by His infinite mercy. Paul writes, "He saved us, not on the basis of deeds which we have done in righteousness, but according to His mercy" (Titus 3:5). "Mercy" (Greek *eleos*) refers to His heartfelt pity toward those in great affliction. This mercy moves Him with compassion to provide relief for sinners in their distress. The apostle Paul teaches that the entire work of salvation, from foreknowledge to glorification, can be encapsulated as "the mercies of God" (Rom. 12:1). Salvation is only possible for spiritually dead sinners because God is "rich in mercy" (Eph. 2:4). He freely bestows His saving grace on spiritual corpses lying in the iron-clad grave of their sin.

In the parable of the prodigal son, Jesus said the father "felt compassion for him, and ran and embraced him and kissed him" (Luke 15:20). "To feel compassion" (Greek *splanchnizomai*) means "to feel something deeply in the pit of the stomach." The noun form (*splanchna*) literally refers to the intestines or bowels of a person. The language is used figuratively to represent deep-seated, gripping emotions. Like the prodigal's father, God feels deeply for sinners in their fallen misery. What He feels for sinners is, as it were, in the very core of His being.

The apostle Peter recognizes the mercy of God to be the ever-flowing fountain from which His salvation flows. He writes: "Blessed be the God and Father of our Lord Jesus Christ, who according to His great mercy has caused us to be born again to a living hope through the resurrection of Jesus Christ from the dead" (1 Peter 1:3). In this doxology, Peter praises God for His "great [Greek *polys*] mercy"—His enormous compassion that is full of magnanimity. Sinners have the greatest need to be saved from divine wrath. This great mercy moves God to provide His salvation for those who are helpless to save themselves.

GOD IS CHOOSING

Saving grace was first activated by God in eternity past through His sovereign will, a truth we explored more fully in a previous chapter. The apostle Paul writes, "Just as He chose us in Him before the foundation of the world, that we would be holy and blameless before Him. In love He predestined us to adoption as sons through Jesus Christ to Himself, according to the kind intention of His will, to the praise of the glory of His grace, which He freely bestowed on us in the Beloved" (Eph. 1:4–6). Before time began, God chose out of the fallen human race those whom He would save.

Paul later writes, God "has saved us . . . according to His own purpose and grace which was granted us in Christ Jesus from all eternity" (2 Tim. 1:9). From long ago, God purposed to bestow His grace on unworthy sinners, not on the basis of anything good in the person chosen. Instead, each is elected by God on the basis of being in the Lord Jesus Christ. Because of the life and death of the Son of God, they are accepted by the Father.

In eternity past, God made a distinguishing choice among fallen sinners in the human race. God chose to fix His heart of love on His elect Bride. He sovereignly purposed to save these sinners because of His undeserved grace. No one can make even the slightest claim that they are owed the electing grace of God. Because such a divine choice is unmerited, God is free, according to His manifold wisdom, to give His grace to whomever He wills. Or He may withhold it from whomever among the guilty. God has chosen whom He will save by His perfect, "gracious choice" (Rom. 11:5).

GOD IS CALLING

Those whom God chose in eternity past, He calls to Himself within time. On the day of Pentecost, Peter declared that the promise of salvation belongs to "as many as the Lord our God will call to Himself" (Acts 2:39). This is the irresistible call of

God that is *effectual,* meaning it will also always be effective in securing its divinely intended results. Those who respond with faith in Christ are "the called of Jesus Christ" (Rom. 1:6). All who are "predestined" are "called according to His purpose" (Rom. 8:28–29). Those whom He foreknew are "called" into saving faith in Jesus Christ (v. 30). Those who were chosen believe "because of Him who calls" (Rom. 9:11). These who are "called" are "not from among Jews only, but also from among Gentiles" (v. 24). This "calling of God" is "irrevocable" (Rom. 11:29)—it can never be rescinded, repeated, or reversed.

All who are called by God will believe in Jesus Christ. They are "saints by calling" (1 Cor. 1:2). Paul explains, "God is faithful, through whom you were called into fellowship with His Son, Jesus Christ" (v. 9). This call is so powerful that it apprehends the one summoned and brings them into relationship with Christ. Those who believe the gospel are "the called" (v. 24). Though they are overlooked by the world, their eternal "calling" reveals they are precious to God (v. 26).

GOD IS REGENERATING

Those whom God effectually calls to Himself, He sovereignly regenerates and births into His kingdom. Those who are made alive in Him are the ones who believe in Jesus Christ (John 11:26). Those who are dead in trespasses and sin (Eph. 2:1) are raised to believe (vv. 5–9). The spiritually dead have no moral ability to believe. But when they are resurrected with new life, they are given the gift of faith and enabled to believe in Jesus Christ (v. 8). To them "it has been granted for Christ's sake . . . to believe in Him" (Phil. 1:29). To them, "Jesus [is] the author and perfecter of faith" (Heb. 12:2). They "have received a faith" (2 Peter 1:1) from God that they did not previously possess.

This divine work of regenerating grace is exclusively a monergistic, or singular act of God. The apostle John explains that believers, "who were born, not of blood nor of the will of the flesh nor of the will of man, but of God" (John 1:13). The new birth is not caused by human lineage, human activity, or human choice, but is exclusively by God's choice and activity. Jesus clarifies: "The wind blows where it wishes and you hear the sound of it, but do not know where it comes from and where it is going; so is everyone who is born of the Spirit" (John 3:8). Regeneration is entirely a saving work of the sovereign grace of God, independent of man.

James writes, "In the exercise of His will He brought us forth by the word of truth, so that we would be a kind of first fruits among His creatures" (James 1:18). The new birth is initiated by the life-giving act of God's will, not man's will. John states, "Whoever believes that Jesus is the Christ is born of God, and whoever loves the Father loves the child born of Him" (1 John 5:1). Everyone who "believes" in Jesus Christ does so because they have been "born of Him" from above.

GOD IS JUSTIFYING

God's grace justifies those who are condemned under His law, when they place their trust in Jesus Christ. Believers are "justified as a gift by His grace through the redemption which is in Christ Jesus" (Rom. 3:24). No one is good enough to deserve His grace. It is bestowed freely on those who do not deserve it. No amount of good works, great or small, can purchase the eternal salvation they desperately need. To be justified is to have stood guilty before the judgment bar of heaven, but be declared righteous by God because of personal faith in the Lord Jesus Christ (Phil. 3:9).

The apostle Paul writes, "For we maintain that a man is justified by faith apart from works of the Law" (Rom. 3:28). When men and women repent of their sins and believe in Jesus Christ as Lord and Savior, the divine Judge of heaven and earth declares them to be right before Him. In this forensic act, God imputes the perfect righteousness of Christ to the one who believes. The apostle Paul writes, "Therefore, having been justified by faith, we have peace with God through our Lord Jesus Christ" (Rom. 5:1). In that decisive moment, the believer in Jesus Christ is freely justified by God (Rom. 8:33). The nakedness of their sin is clothed by God with the pure white robes of Jesus' perfect righteousness. This gift is given to those who by their nature and deeds stand condemned under the divine law. This new status of "no condemnation" (Rom. 8:1) is received by faith alone in Christ alone. That person is irrevocably declared justified as a gift of His grace.

As the Great Physician, Jesus did not come for those who believe they are spiritually well. Instead, He came for those who are sick and dying from the deadly plague of sin. Jesus says: "It is not those who are well who need a physician, but those who are sick. I have not come to call the righteous but sinners to repentance" (Luke 5:31–32). All the world is diagnosed as being in desperate need of His righteousness. Those who claim to be righteous in their own merit will never receive the righteousness of God. Only those who confess their own sin before God will be "justified" and receive the imputation of divine righteousness (Luke 18:14).

GOD IS RESCUING

The grace of God rescues those who are perishing in their sins (John 3:16). The apostle Paul writes, "He [God] rescued us from the domain of darkness, and transferred us to the kingdom of His beloved Son" (Col. 1:13). The word "rescued" (Greek *rhuomai*) means "to draw to oneself, to save from danger." God saves from eternal destruction those who cannot save themselves. They are delivered from the clutches of Satan's power. The death of Jesus Christ crushed the head of the serpent (Gen. 3:15) and delivered captives out of his kingdom of darkness and into the glorious light of God (John 3:19–21).

Believers are "saved through the grace of the Lord Jesus" (Acts 15:11) as God acts in a twofold manner. On one side, divine salvation delivers believing sinners *from* "the domain of darkness" (Col. 1:13), *from* eternal destruction and damnation. On the other side, the believer is "transferred" *to* "the kingdom of His beloved Son." Paul writes: "For by grace you have been saved through faith; and that not of yourselves, it is the gift of God" (Eph. 2:8). Those who repent and believe are "saved from the wrath of God" (Rom. 5:9) in the flames of hell. Succinctly stated, they are saved *from* God's wrath *by* God's grace, *for* God's glory.

"Saved" (Greek *sōzō*), a frequently used word in the New Testament, means "to be delivered from danger or destruction." It represents being rescued from eternal peril. Believers have been saved from the coming wrath of God, by His grace, through the work of the Lord Jesus Christ. Paul writes, "Being justified by His grace we would be made heirs according to the hope of eternal life" (Titus 3:7). Though none deserve to receive His salvation, God bestows it without cost or merit. This truly is amazing grace.

GOD IS FORGIVING

The saving grace of God is also distinguished by the full and free forgiveness He gives to those who are guilty offenders under His law. God said that He "forgives iniquity, transgression and sin" (Ex. 34:7). The Hebrew word for "forgiveness" (*nasa*) means "to lift up, to take away." In divine forgiveness, God lifts the heavy guilt of sin off the sinner and places it on an innocent sin-bearer, Jesus Christ, who carries it far away (John 1:29). The threefold designation of sin—"iniquity, transgression and sin"—emphasizes the enormity of the many sins that God forgives. He is a "God of forgiveness" (Neh. 9:17), who is ready to pardon the innumerable iniquities we commit against Him.

David writes: "How blessed is he whose transgression is forgiven, whose sin is covered! How blessed is the man to whom the LORD does not impute iniquity" (Ps. 32:1–2). David marvels that sins are "forgiven" (Hebrew *nasa*) and "covered" (Hebrew *kasah*, "to have sin concealed") and that God "does not impute" (Hebrew *hashab*) or "charge to" our indebted accounts. This speaks to the magnitude of God's forgiving grace. David wrote, "For You, Lord, are good, and ready to forgive" (Ps. 86:5). This stresses the full and final cancellation of our sin debt when God sends away the penalty of a person's sin against Him.

The psalmist extolls God, "If You, LORD, should mark iniquities, O Lord, who could stand? But there is forgiveness with You" (Ps. 130:3–4). If God should hold our sin against us, none could stand with acceptance before Him. But there *is* forgiveness with God, which gives a standing of acceptance before Him. Again, David writes, "As far as the east is from the west, so far has He removed our transgressions from us" (Ps. 103:12). The distance from the east to the west cannot be measured. How vast and infinite is the Lord's forgiveness of our sins!

In the New Testament, the apostle Paul writes, "In [Christ] we have redemption . . . the forgiveness of our trespasses" (Eph. 1:7). All forgiveness by God is realized by virtue of the saving work of Christ. In Greek, "to forgive" (*aphiēmi*) means "to send away, to send forth." God is faithful to His promise to send away the sins of believers in Jesus Christ. This pardon is the costly result of the sin-bearing death of Christ upon the cross (Eph. 1:7). The apostle John states that God is "faithful and righteous to forgive us our sins and to cleanse us from all unrighteousness" (1 John 1:9). The blood of Christ washes away every sin in the life of the true believer.

GOD IS REDEEMING

By His saving grace, God is also the Redeemer of His people. God repeatedly declares, "Your Redeemer is the Holy One of Israel" (Isa. 41:14; cf. 43:14; 48:17–19; 49:7; 54:5). "Redeemer" (*gaal*) is the Hebrew word for a near relative who has the opportunity to buy back a possession another relative has lost. As our Redeemer, Jesus Christ has paid the price to purchase lost sinners from perishing through the shedding of His blood on the cross. The "Redeemer, the LORD of hosts," says: "I have wiped out your transgressions like a thick cloud and your sins like a heavy mist. Return to Me, for I have redeemed you" (Isa. 44:6, 22). The redemption that God provides is through the blood of the pursuing kinsman Redeemer, Jesus Christ Himself.

In the New Testament, the apostle Paul describes this saving act accomplished by Jesus Christ: "We have redemption through

His blood, the forgiveness of our trespasses, according to the riches of His grace" (Eph. 1:7). Here, the word "redemption" (Greek *apolutrōsis*) means "the payment of a ransom to secure the deliverance of one held captive." It represents a person paying the price to secure the freedom of another person who is in bondage to slavery. Even so, the death of Christ paid the price for all those who believe in Him. He bought them out of the slave market of sin and set them free through His wondrous grace (John 8:36).

The apostle Peter confirms this truth: "You were not redeemed with perishable things like silver or gold from your futile way of life inherited from your forefathers, but with precious blood, as of a lamb unblemished and spotless, the blood of Christ" (1 Peter 1:18–19). The term "redeemed" (Greek *lutroō*) means "to ransom" or "to deliver by the payment of a price." The purchase price of the redemption of sinners, held captive by their sins, was the blood of Jesus Christ shed on the cross (Titus 2:14). By making this payment to God, His death secured the release of all those for whom He died.

GOD IS SANCTIFYING

Inseparably connected to God's justifying grace is His sanctifying grace. These two divine acts can never be separated (1 Cor. 1:30). This life-changing work of God in sanctification, Paul writes, transforms believers into "the image of His Son" (Rom. 8:29). Spiritual growth always follows God's regenerating work. The apostle explains, "It is God who is at work in you, both to will and to work for His good pleasure" (Phil. 2:13). The sanctifying activity of God in His saints conforms them "according to the image of the One who created him" (Col. 3:10). Despite believers' ongoing struggle with sin (Rom. 7:14–21), God gives a far greater grace to overcome sin's power. His all-sufficient grace enables every child of God to resist temptation, flee immorality, and pursue holiness. Every believer experiences "grace upon grace" (John 1:16) as they "are being transformed into the same image from glory to glory" (2 Cor. 3:18). Throughout the Christian life, God's "grace" is being "multiplied" (2 Peter 1:2), giving "divine power" for "everything pertaining to life and godliness" (v. 3).

God gives abundant grace to live the Christian life. This divine empowerment provides the supernatural strength needed to pursue God-honoring holiness (2 Cor. 12:9). Sanctifying grace makes us strong in every circumstance of life. This enabling grace allows us to do whatever God calls us to. He bestows His transforming grace that energizes us to minister in His name (1 Peter 4:10). The testimony of every believer is the same as that of the apostle Paul: "By the grace of God I am what I am" (1 Cor. 15:10). God will provide this grace all the way to the last day of our lives, so that we may remain strong in our hope in Christ.

GOD IS GLORIFYING

In every believer, God will complete His work of grace throughout eternity future. The apostle Paul writes, "For I am confident of this very thing, that He who began a good work in you will perfect it until the day of Christ Jesus" (Phil. 1:6). Whenever God begins a work of saving grace in a person, He will always finish what He starts. "The day of Christ Jesus" is the final day at the end of the age, when Christ will return. At that time, God will glorify believers, transforming them completely into the full likeness of Christ, as much as a redeemed saint can be.

Concerning this final work of grace, Paul writes, "These whom He predestined, He also called; and these whom He called, He also justified; and these whom He justified, He also glorified" (Rom. 8:30). Paul stated this in the past tense—"glorified"—to emphasize its certainty. It is as though this concluding stage of grace has already occurred in the mind of God. God will surely glorify in eternal future all whom He "has chosen" in eternity past and "called" within time (2 Thess. 2:13–14).

ALL OF GRACE

As we have seen, the salvation of undeserving sinners is all of grace. From start to finish, "salvation belongs to the LORD" (Ps. 3:8). From eternity past to eternity future, this divine work of rescuing sinners is entirely on the basis of grace (2 Tim. 1:9). Their only contribution is the sin that was laid on Jesus Christ. Even repentance and faith are gifts of grace, bestowed by God on those whom He purposes to save (Acts 11:18).

Therefore, all glory goes to God, because all grace is from Him (Eph. 1:6, 12, 14). Every aspect of His saving grace is reason for us to praise His glorious name (Rom. 11:36). God alone deserves our worship because He alone has delivered us from our ruin in sin. This gracious Lord is the One who has raised us to newness of life. To Him be the glory forever—amen.

Chapter Sixteen

UNCONDITIONALLY LOVING

The Love of God

God does not love us because we are valuable,
but we are valuable because God loves us.

—Martin Luther

O ne key attribute of God we have yet to explore is undoubt-edly the most cherished. I refer to the love of God, which is surely the most beloved aspect of the divine character. The love of God has comforted troubled hearts in the darkest storms of life. It has lifted spirits that have sunk into the lowest valleys of despair. This profound truth has brought the greatest encouragement to those who have lost hope.

Yet, no divine attribute has been more misunderstood than the love of God. Too often, it is seen as a mere mushy, sentimental feeling, but nothing could be farther from the truth. While divine love does involve His tender feelings toward us, it runs much deeper and involves much more of His divine being. Seen from a higher vantage point, divine love is a strong commitment by the sovereign will of God toward sinful men and women whom He has chosen for salvation. Far more than a fluctuating whim, the love of God is rooted and grounded in the eternal counsel of His divine will.

In the New Testament, the strongest Greek word for "love" is *agapē*, which is most commonly used to describe the perfection of divine love. This word represents the highest level of love, that steadfast commitment of God toward His people, anchored in the immutability of His divine character. It is unfathomable that the love of God, unchanging and ever strong, would reach down to such defiled sinners who fall short of His glory. God has chosen to set His love on a vast multitude in this fallen human race, though they are wretched by nature.

In this chapter, we will consider different aspects of His divine love that will help us better understand the wonder of this reality. Here is God's determinative will and affectionate heart for those upon whom He chooses to set His saving grace.

GOD IS LOVE

The Bible teaches that the very nature of God is love. The apostle John declares, "God is love" (1 John 4:8). In other words, the entire being of God is permeated with love. Divine love is inseparably connected with every other attribute that He possesses. That is, His love is holy love—pure and flawless—because God is also holy. His love is immutable—never changing—because God Himself is also immutable. The love of God is filled with His omnipotence, strengthening His children, because He is all-powerful. God's love is sovereign love, because He possesses supreme authority, which is seen in His choosing to love His elect.

It is eternal love, beginning before the foundation of the world, because He is without beginning—and continuing on without end. It is righteous love, always doing what is right. This love of God is inseparably interwoven with every other divine attribute in His glorious essence. It is endless, boundless, bottomless.

God loves individuals not because of their loveliness—which none have because of their sin—but because He Himself is love. The reason for His love arises from within Himself, not from anything inherently attractive in the ones who are loved. God loves not because of the goodness of the individual loved, but in spite of his many sins. He loves because it is His very nature to love those who are unlovely.

GOD IS SELF-LOVING

The love of God strongly exists between the three persons of the Trinity. God the Father has loved God the Son from "before the foundation of the world" (John 17:24). The Son likewise was "in the bosom of the Father" from before time began (John 1:18). This expresses the intimate love relationship between the Father and the Son. It is as though the Son was laying His head on the bosom of the Father in closest relational communion. This same perfect love is shown by the Father and the Son to the Holy Spirit. In turn, the Spirit loves the Father and the Son. Between the three persons of the Godhead, there exists perfect, eternal love.

When Jesus was baptized during the days of His earthly ministry, the heavens opened and God the Father said, "This is My beloved Son, in whom I am well-pleased" (Matt. 3:17). Here was openly announced the greatness of the Father's love for His Son. Jesus later said, "The Father loves the Son and has given all things into His hand" (John 3:35). On another occasion, Jesus confidently asserted, "The Father loves Me, because I lay down My life so that I may take it again" (John 10:17). The Son did His Father's will, to the delight of the Father.

In the Upper Room, Jesus told His disciples, "The Father has loved Me" (John 15:9). In turn, Jesus expressed, "I have kept My Father's commandments and abide in His love" (v. 10). Jesus said, "So that the world may know that I love the Father, I do exactly as the Father commanded Me" (John 14:31). It was the Son's obedience to the Father that demonstrated His love for Him. In His High Priestly Prayer, Jesus confessed to the Father, "You have loved Me" (John 17:23). Jesus again acknowledged the reality of "the love with which You loved Me" (v. 26).

GOD IS INITIATING

This divine love between the persons of the Trinity overflows toward unworthy sinners. The apostle Paul wrote: "He chose us in Him before the foundation of the world, that we would be holy and blameless before Him. In love He predestined us to adoption as sons" (Eph. 1:4–5). Divine love motivated the Father to choose His elect before time began. God the Father then gave His elect to His Son to be His chosen bride (John 6:37, 39; 10:29; 17:2, 6, 9, 24). This was a superlative expression of His love. God said, "I have loved you with an everlasting love" (Jer. 31:3). Some people think of predestination as a harsh truth, but it is an expression of God's immeasurable love toward His people.

God loves His elect because He chose to love them. Moses said, "The LORD did not set His love on you nor choose you because you were more in number than any of the peoples, for you were the fewest of all peoples, but because the LORD loved you" (Deut. 7:7–8). God did not love His sinful creatures because there was anything inherently good in them. This divine love self-originated in God's own character, because He is love. The apostle John wrote, "In this is love, not that we loved God, but that He loved us" (1 John 4:10). "We love, because He first loved us" (v. 19). God is the great Author in loving His chosen ones. As an act of His sovereign will, God long ago set His heart on His elect, to bring them into the amazing wonder of His redemptive love.

GOD IS MERCIFUL

A critical aspect of the love of God is His mercy. Concerning this facet of divine love, David reflects, "His mercies are great" (2 Sam. 24:14). "Mercies" translates the Hebrew word *rahamim*, which speaks of the bowels or intestines. It represents the deep affections of God toward His chosen ones.

Zacharias spoke of "the tender mercy of our God" (Luke 1:78). Divine "mercy" (Greek *eleos*) stresses how kindly God looks upon sinners in their miserable, pitiful plight caused by their sins. Mercy stirs God to rescue perishing souls in their helpless state. Mercy draws Him to show compassion toward those in their desperate condition in order to remedy it. Mercy moves God to be grieved over the ruined sinner's disposition of despair in his sin. Here is the intensity of God's loving concern for sinners. It describes the tenderhearted motives behind God's granting eternal life to believers. Out of His limitless mercy, He chose to grant salvation of His own accord.

The apostle Paul writes of "the mercies of God" (Rom. 12:1). This includes all the saving graces of God, from foreknowledge and predestination to glorification (Rom. 8:29–30). He identifies God the Father as "the Father of mercies" (2 Cor. 1:3). He also wrote that God is "rich in mercy" (Eph. 2:4). That God is "rich" (Greek *plousios*) indicates that He has vast, immeasurable oceans of mercy to bestow upon His loved ones. Peter states, "His great mercy has caused us to be born again" (1 Peter 1:3). Time and time again, Scripture attests to the greatness of God's loving mercy.

GOD IS COMPASSIONATE

Yet another aspect of the love of God is the compassion He lavishes on sinners. It is His deep compassion that moves Him to rescue those suffering in their desperation. This aspect of divine love is exercised toward His elect. God said, "I . . . will show compassion on whom I will show compassion" (Ex. 33:19). To "show compassion" (Hebrew *raham*) means "to love deeply, to have tender affection." Moses said, "The LORD your God will restore you from captivity, and have compassion on you" (Deut. 30:3). It was said that God possesses "great compassion" (Neh. 9:19). Isaiah said, "The LORD will have compassion on Jacob" (Isa. 14:1). Jeremiah writes, "His compassions never fail" (Lam. 3:22). Jesus "felt compassion for them because they were like sheep without a shepherd" (Mark 6:34). James writes, "the Lord is full of compassion" (James 5:11). These verses bear clear testimony to the compassion of God.

In the New Testament, the Greek word for "compassion" (*splanchna*) literally refers to the inner parts of the body, especially the intestines or bowels. It could also refer to the heart, liver, or lungs. Figuratively speaking, it was used to describe deeply felt emotions toward those who find themselves in dire need. In other words, it meant to feel something in the pit of one's stomach. It meant to be moved with deep feelings for someone suffering in dire straits. As it relates to God, compassion represents His genuine care for perishing sinners who are self-destructing in their sin.

GOD IS AFFECTIONATE

The love of God is more than the volitional choice of His will in sovereign election. It also includes the burning passion that He feels for His people. God is not a stoic sovereign, only making rational decisions that are devoid of any affections. The love of God runs much deeper than merely making cold, cerebral choices toward His elect. Moses affirms the same: "The LORD will again rejoice over you" (Deut. 30:9). Isaiah announces, "The LORD delights in you. . . . As the bridegroom rejoices over the bride, so your God will rejoice over you" (Isa. 62:4–5). God said, "I will . . . be glad in My people" (Isa. 65:19). Again, "I will rejoice over them to do them good" (Jer. 32:41). Such divine love is full of the strong emotion of God's rejoicing over His people. The prophet Zephaniah declares that "the LORD your God . . . will exult over you with joy . . . He will rejoice over you with shouts of joy" (Zeph. 3:17). Here is the heart of God, full of fervent affection for His chosen ones.

Describing the depth of love God has for His people, Jesus told a parable about a shepherd who searches for a lost sheep until he finally finds it. When he rescues the lost sheep, he greatly rejoices over it. In the same way, God is exuberant when He saves even one sinner from perishing (Luke 15:1–7). When the Father calls His lost sheep to Himself, it is not merely an impersonal legal transaction that occurs in heaven. Rather, God is overjoyed whenever He brings anyone to faith in His Son, the Lord Jesus Christ.

Jesus told another parable about a prodigal son who demanded the share of his inheritance, but squandered it in a far country (Luke 15:11–32). When the son came to his senses, he determined he would return to his father. When the father saw him coming, he "felt compassion for him" (v. 20), meaning that he was deeply moved with pity for his wayward son. He ran to meet him and smothered him with kisses. The father shouted, "Quickly bring out the best robe and put it on him, and put a ring on his hand and sandals on his feet; and bring the fattened calf, kill it, and let us eat and celebrate" (vv. 22–23). Likewise, there is a celebration in the heart of God over the salvation of those who come to Him by faith.

GOD IS KIND

Moreover, the love of God also includes His divine kindness. Paul asked, "Do you think lightly of the riches of His kindness?" (Rom. 2:4). The apostle also wrote, "Behold then the kindness . . . of God" (Rom. 11:22). He further spoke of "the surpassing riches of His grace in kindness toward us in Christ Jesus" (Eph. 2:7). Again, Paul elaborated on "when the kindness of God our Savior and His love for mankind appeared" (Titus 3:4). These verses stress the remarkable kindness with which God has dealt with sinners.

Divine kindness (Greek *chrēstotes*) represents the genuine goodness of God's heart toward sinners in need of His grace. Kindness refers to His gracious concern that led Him to redeem us from our sins. It is the nature of God to be kind to the abysmally lost. Jesus said that "the Most High . . . is kind to ungrateful and evil men" (Luke 6:35). It is the kindness of God that initiates drawing sinners to Himself and granting them repentance and saving faith. "The kindness of God leads you to repentance" (Rom. 2:4) and bestows the benefits He gives to those in need of His grace.

GOD IS SACRIFICIAL

The love of God is a sacrificial love that gives at great personal cost, to seek the highest good of the one loved. More than mere words, God demonstrates His love in actions at great cost to Him. Jesus explains this sacrificial love: "For God so loved the world, that He gave His only begotten Son, that whoever believes in Him shall not perish, but have eternal life" (John 3:16). The point Jesus stresses is upon the Father giving Him, His only begotten Son, to die for rebellious sinners. No greater sacrifice could have been made by the Father than giving His Son upon the cross.

The apostle Paul underscores the same costly sacrifice of the love of God: "God demonstrates His own love toward us, in that while we were yet sinners, Christ died for us" (Rom. 5:8). The focus is directed toward God the Father, who sacrificially gave His Son unto death for sinners. God did more than speak loving words toward undeserving sinners. He did more than simply feel warm compassion for rebels against His law. God decisively made the greatest sacrifice ever demonstrated by sending His Son to die on the cross.

Likewise, no greater love could have been expressed by Jesus toward sinners than to die for them. He said, "Greater love has no one than this, that one lay down his life for his friends" (John 15:13). Jesus gave the supreme demonstration of His sacrificial love at the cross.

GOD IS JEALOUS

Another essential aspect of the love of God is His jealousy. In issuing the Ten Commandments, God says, "You shall have no other gods before Me" (Ex. 20:3). By this imperative, no other person or object, whether real or imagined, may be tolerated in place of or in opposition to the one true God. The Lord then added, "I, the LORD your God, am a jealous God" (v. 5). Moses again states, "You shall not worship any other god, for the LORD, whose name is Jealous, is a jealous God" (Ex. 34:14). With a holy jealousy, God demands to be adored exclusively and preeminently by His loved ones. The prophet Nahum records, "A jealous and avenging God is the LORD" (Nah. 1:2). This announces that God must be worshiped with supreme affection. Otherwise, His jealousy will be provoked.

The intense jealousy of God's love is aroused whenever anyone or anything is made the chief affection of a person's life. When the law was reissued, Moses states, "For the LORD your God is a consuming fire, a jealous God" (Deut. 4:24). The jealousy of God causes Him to be fiercely protective of the supreme allegiance that is due Him. When Joshua addressed the nation of Israel, he made the same declaration: "He is a holy God. He is a jealous God" (Josh. 24:19). Divine jealousy demands supreme loyalty from His people.

GOD IS CHASTENING

When God's children live in disobedience, He lovingly disciplines them for their spiritual good. Solomon records, "My son, do not reject the discipline of the LORD or loathe His reproof, for whom the LORD loves He reproves, even as a father corrects the son in whom he delights" (Prov. 3:11–12). A father's love without correcting his son through discipline is not true love. The one who genuinely loves seeks the highest good of the one loved, which necessitates that he admonish and chastise his children when they sin. Consequently, every child of God who is the object of the Father's love receives His chastening discipline.

This same truth is reaffirmed in the New Testament when the author of Hebrews writes: "It is for discipline that you endure; God deals with you as with sons; for what son is there whom his father does not discipline?" (Heb. 12:7). This rhetorical question implies the obvious answer that no loving father would withhold discipline from the son whom he loves. In like manner, neither does our heavenly Father hold back His corrective discipline from His own children. For us to be without His discipline would mean we would be an illegitimate son or daughter.

The author of Hebrews explains the reason for God's discipline: "He disciplines us for our good, so that we may share His holiness" (Heb. 12:10). The purpose of divine discipline is not for God to harm His children. Rather, God chastens His spiritual offspring to mature them in their growth in godliness. God's discipline is an indispensable part of His gracious love for those born again and adopted into His family. God loves them unconditionally as they are. But He cares for His children too much to allow them to remain as they are, especially whenever they lapse into prolonged disobedience.

GOD IS STEADFAST

The love of God is steadfast toward those whom He has chosen and called to Himself. Those upon whom He set His heart in eternity past, He will continue to love into eternity future. Twenty-six times in Psalm 136, one time per verse, we read, "His loving-kindness is everlasting." This is to say, nothing could ever cause God to annul the loyal love of His commitment to any believer. The word translated "lovingkindness" (Hebrew *hesed*) is His loyal, unconditional love by which he binds Himself to His people with an irrevocable allegiance. Nothing could cause Him to forfeit His love toward a person whom He loved in eternity past. His love is too strong and deep to ever cease.

The apostle Paul affirms this truth: "For I am convinced that neither death, nor life, nor angels, nor principalities, nor things present, nor things to come, nor powers, nor height, nor depth, nor any other created thing, will be able to separate us from the love of God, which is in Christ Jesus our Lord" (Rom. 8:38–39). The love of God toward His elect will never be extinguished in the present time or throughout the ages to come. God will never love someone only to later rescind His love. Once a person is loved by God, that individual will forever be loved by Him.

IMMERSED IN GOD'S LOVE

As we go about life's duties, let us never lose sight of the fact that we are immersed in the bottomless ocean of God's love. We are surrounded by His tender mercy toward us on every side. God is constantly caring for us to meet our every true need. Even when we are unaware of His loving support, He nevertheless remains present to attend to our every need. Even when we become self-reliant and self-absorbed, nothing cancels out His constant provision and protection.

We are aware of only a small portion of what God is doing at any one moment in our lives. Too often, it is only in times of adversity that we call on Him for His help. But every moment of every day, God is working to cause all things to work together for our good (Rom. 8:28). Even when we are faithless, He remains faithful (2 Tim. 2:13). When we drift from Him who is our first love, He remains steadfast in His love toward us and calls us back (Rev. 2:4–5). His fervent devotion toward us is like a raging fire that cannot be extinguished.

In the midst of our busy lives, let us never lose sight of God's constant care for us. His love never stops giving to meet our needs. He is always going *ahead* of us to prepare the way. He comes *behind* us to protect us. He is *under* us to support us. He is *beside* us to encourage us. He is *in* us to strengthen us. We are forever immersed in "the breadth and length and height and depth" (Eph. 3:18) of His great and glorious love.

Chapter Seventeen

SOVEREIGNLY SELECTING

The Foreknowledge of God

It is not our choice of God that matters,
but rather God's choice of us.

—James Montgomery Boice

Many if not most people assume that divine foreknowledge means God's foresight of future events. Sadly, foreknowledge must be the most misunderstood attribute of God. Some believe that this aspect of God means simply that He is looking down the proverbial tunnel of time to see what decision people will make concerning His Son, Jesus Christ. Based on what God foresees, He will respond by choosing to save those whom He discovers choosing His Son. They understand God's choice to be dependent on man's will.

In this seemingly logical scenario, every individual determines His own destiny. God is merely waiting to see what decision each person will make. Whatever a person chooses, God is rubber-stamping that decision. In this view, God is following man's choice—not the other way around. In this scheme, man is in the front seat behind the steering wheel, driving his own destiny—and God is in the back seat merely looking out the window at unfolding events.

However, this way of looking at divine foreknowledge is entirely false. It is usually based on a well-known passage of Scripture in Paul's letter to the Romans: "For those whom He foreknew, He also predestined to become conformed to the image of His Son, so that He would be the firstborn among many brethren; and these whom He predestined, He also called; and these whom He called, He also justified; and these whom He justified, He also glorified" (Rom. 8:29–30). A particular understanding of these verses assumes that foreknowledge means foresight. In other words, God only predestines what He foresees man doing.

I know this position well because I once held it. It was not until I began to study the Scriptures more carefully that I saw its fallacy. My mishandling of Scripture was due to a lack of knowledge of the Bible, both linguistically and theologically. Unknowingly, my faulty position was robbing God of His glory—something I would never intentionally do. But I was doing it nonetheless. My misinterpretation elevated man to an enthroned position that belongs exclusively to God. I was 180 degrees opposite of what the Bible teaches.

I want to help you avoid the mistake I made. I want to show why this foresight interpretation collapses under the weight of a more careful inspection of the Scripture. Then I will give you the proper interpretation of this divine attribute. To begin with, there are four major reasons why the foresight view is far from the biblical truth.

GOD NEVER LEARNS ANYTHING

The first reason this is incorrect is that God has never looked into the future and learned anything. Since God is omniscient, He knows all things eternally and immediately. He has never peered into time and learned anything unknown to Him. God never looks into the distant horizon of time and discovers what He did not previously know. In actuality, the only thing God foresees is what He has already foreordained before the foundation of the world.

God says that He stands at the beginning and declares the end from the beginning: "Remember the former things long past, for I am God, and there is no other; I am God, and there is no one like Me, declaring the end from the beginning, and from ancient times things which have not been done, saying, 'My purpose will be established, and I will accomplish all My good pleasure'; calling a bird of prey from the east, the man of My purpose from a far country. Truly I have spoken; truly I will bring it to pass. I have planned it, surely I will do it" (Isa. 46:9–11). God does not merely observe the end from the beginning; He *declares* it. This means that before time began, He sovereignly declared that the future would come to pass.

ALL GOD SEES IS UNBELIEF

The second reason that this foresight view is incorrect is because if all God did was look into the future, all He would see is that *no one* would believe in Jesus Christ. The total depravity of the human heart includes the bondage of the will. No one can choose to believe in Jesus Christ by his own initiative or will. Repeatedly, Scripture teaches that repentance and saving faith are gifts that God must give to the guilty sinner before he can embrace Jesus

Christ as Savior and Lord (Acts 11:18; Eph. 2:8–9; Phil. 1:29; Heb. 12:2; 2 Peter 1:1; 1 John 5:1). A dead man has no ability to do anything toward God. Such a spiritual corpse cannot believe in Jesus Christ.

Isaiah records, "All of us like sheep have gone astray, each of us has turned to his own way" (Isa. 53:6). John explains that people are born again not by "the will of man, but of God" (John 1:13). Jesus teaches, "No one can come to Me" (John 6:44; cf. v. 65). Here is man's moral inability to come to Jesus. Paul explains the moral inability of the unconverted sinner: "There is none who understands, there is none who seeks for God" (Rom. 3:11). "So then it does not depend on the man who wills or the man who runs, but on God who has mercy" (Rom. 9:16). This is why no one has free will to believe on his own.

FOREKNOWLEDGE INVOLVES PEOPLE

The third reason foreknowledge does not mean "foresight" is because a careful distinction needs to be made in Romans 8:29. In describing foreknowledge, Paul uses the personal pronoun *whom*, not the impersonal pronoun *what*. This verse says, "For those whom He foreknew." This does not say God is foreseeing *events*, such as faith being exercised in Christ. If that was intended, this passage would read "*what* He foresaw." Rather, he intentionally writes "*whom* He foreknew," which refers to individuals. In this passage, Paul is addressing God's relationship with *individuals*, not incidents.

FOREKNOWN MEANS FORE-LOVED

The fourth reason the foresight view is faulty is it shows a lack of understanding of what the word "foreknowledge" (Greek *proginōskō*) actually means. In the original Greek language, the word "foreknowledge" is a compound word. The main verb is *ginōskō*, which means "to know someone in a personal relationship" (John 10:14, 27). It is synonymous with loving another person in an intimate way (1 Cor. 8:3). In Scripture, "to know" is often used to refer to the sexual relationship between a husband and a wife. This degree of loving intimacy is what it is for a husband to know his wife. The prefix is *pro,* which means "before, beforehand." When these two words are combined, *proginōskō* means "to love someone beforehand" (see Rom. 11:2).

This being so, Paul uses "foreknowledge" to mean "those whom God *previously chose to love with a special, distinguishing love.*" This word refers to those individuals whom God purposed to love before the foundation of the world (1 Peter 1:2). This divine love was based on nothing lovable in the one chosen. This love originated in Him for reasons known only to Himself. He loved those whom He chose to love simply because He chose to do so.

In order to best understand the foreknowledge of God, we want to survey the Bible to grasp a proper understanding of its meaning. Divine foreknowledge involves the following aspects.

GOD IS PRE-LOVING

The first use of the concept of "knowing" in the Scripture is found in the fourth chapter of the Bible: "Now the man had relations with his wife Eve, and she conceived and gave birth to Cain" (Gen. 4:1). The Hebrew equivalent of the Greek word *ginōskō* is *yada.* The words "had relations with" is a discreet way to speak of the sexual union between a man and his wife. This verse literally reads, "The man *knew* his wife, and she conceived and she gave birth." To "know" another person means to love them in the most intimate, exclusive way.

The same Hebrew word (*yada*) is used again a few verses later: "Cain had relations with his wife and she conceived, and gave birth to Enoch" (v. 17). Once more, the text reads, "Adam had relations with his wife again; and she gave birth to a son, and named him Seth" (v. 25). "Had relations with" (*yada*) means "to have close relations with" (see Gen. 24:16; 38:26) or "to love intimately."

The Hebrew word *yada* does not mean "foresight." Eve would have never become pregnant with mere foresight by Adam. Adam had to do more than simply anticipate what she would do. The conception that occurred in her required an intimate love relationship with her husband. So it is that God chose to initiate a saving relationship with His elect.

GOD IS PRE-APPOINTING

We later find the word "know" (*yada*) used synonymously with God's predetermining choice to put Jeremiah into the prophetic office. God said, "Before I formed you in the womb I knew [*yada*] you, and before you were born I consecrated you; I have appointed you a prophet to the nations" (Jer. 1:5). God states that He "knew" Jeremiah before he was born. This does not mean that God merely knew *about* him. That fact should be obvious given divine omniscience. Rather, "before" Jeremiah was formed in the womb, God had already *chosen* him for this assignment.

In like manner, divine foreknowledge means that God appointed His elect to salvation in Jesus Christ before they were conceived in the womb. The determinative choice was made before God formed them in their mother's womb. Luke explains, "As many as had been appointed to eternal life believed" (Acts 13:48). All those previously appointed by God for salvation are those who believe. No more believe, and no fewer believe.

GOD IS PRE-CHOOSING

Elsewhere in the Old Testament, the word "to know" is sometimes used synonymously with "to choose." God spoke to Israel, saying, "You only have I chosen [*yada*] among all the families of the earth" (Amos 3:2). In this passage, the Hebrew word *yada* is translated "known" in some English translations (e.g., ESV, NKJV, KJV) and "chosen" in others (e.g., NASB, NIV). In this context, the most literal translation of this word *yada* is "chosen" (Gen. 18:19). To know someone, biblically speaking, is to choose to love that one. To the nation Israel, God was saying, "Of all the nations of the world, you alone are My chosen people." God chose Israel in a way He did not choose the Egyptians, Babylonians, or Assyrians.

In the New Testament, the word "know" (Greek *ginōskō*) is used the same way. Matthew records: "And Joseph awoke from his sleep and did as the angel the Lord commanded him, and took Mary as his wife, but kept her a virgin [literally, "did not know (*ginōskō*) her"] until she gave birth to a Son" (Matt. 1:24–25). In the original Greek, this passage literally reads, "she was not *known* by Joseph." The word "virgin" does not appear in the original language, though it is traditionally translated as Joseph "kept her a virgin." This literally says that "Joseph never *knew* her" or "she was never *known* by Joseph." For Mary to be a virgin, it meant that she was not yet known by Joseph in an intimate, love relationship.

At the end of the Sermon on the Mount, Jesus concludes:

"Not everyone who says to Me, 'Lord, Lord,' will enter the kingdom of heaven, but he who does the will of My Father who is in heaven will enter. Many will say to Me on that day, 'Lord, Lord, did we not prophesy in Your name, and in Your name cast out demons, and in Your name perform many miracles?' And then I will declare to them, 'I never knew [*ginōskō*] you; depart from Me, you who practice lawlessness'" (Matt. 7:21–23). Granted, Jesus knows everything *about* everyone. But He personally only knows those who were foreknown by the Father. Jesus does not know unbelievers in a saving relationship.

It is clear that the word "foreknowledge" refers to those with whom God chose to enter into a special, saving relationship—before time began. For God to foreknow someone means He chose in eternity past to love them with a saving love. Foreknowledge means they were previously chosen by God.

GOD IS PRE-KNOWING

Jesus further used "know" (*ginōskō*) to mean a personal relationship. He says, "I am the good shepherd, and I know [*ginōskō*] My own and My own know Me" (John 10:14). "Know" means far more than Jesus merely knowing about them. To the contrary, Jesus means, "I have an intimate, saving relationship with My sheep." Jesus declares, "My sheep hear My voice, and I know them, and they follow Me" (v. 27). For Jesus to know His sheep means He has a saving relationship with them. He does not know other sheep that do not belong to Him.

Later, Jesus intercedes, "This is eternal life, that they may know You" (John 17:3). Eternal life is to know God and His Son, Jesus Christ, in a close, personal relationship.

The apostle Paul writes, "If anyone loves God, he is known by Him" (1 Cor. 8:3). Here, "loves" and "is known by" are used interchangeably. To be specific, being known by God (cause) results in the believing sinner's loving Him (result). The apostle elsewhere says to know God is to be known by Him. He writes, "You have come to know God, or rather to be known by God" (Gal. 4:9). Believers know God (result) because they have been known by Him (cause). Later, Paul writes, "The Lord knows those who are His" (2 Tim. 2:19). God only knows those whom He chose to belong to Him.

"Foreknowledge" means those God would enter a loving relationship with are those whom He chose before time began. God set His heart on His elect with a specific, saving love. He purposed to enter into a saving relationship with those whom He chose before the foundation of the world. God permanently wrote their names in the Book of Life, never to be removed. Before time began, those foreknown by the Father were given by Him to Jesus to be His chosen bride. In eternity past, Jesus knew these same individuals as the Father knew them.

GOD IS PRE-DETERMINING

On the day of Pentecost, Peter preached a powerful evangelistic sermon to thousands of unbelieving Jews. Proclaiming Jesus as the risen Savior, he announces, "This Man, delivered over by the predetermined plan and foreknowledge of God" (Acts 2:23). In this statement, the "foreknowledge of God" is used synonymously with His "predetermined plan." In this passage, "foreknowledge" certainly does not mean God the Father looked down the tunnel of time to see what would happen to His Son. God did not unexpectedly learn that Jesus would be nailed to a cross. God did not foresee the crucifixion as an event that grew out of control. God did not suddenly realize He had to cause the death of His Son to adapt to something He never originally intended.

Instead, Peter meant that divine "foreknowledge" was a part of the predetermined plan of God for the death of Christ. God had marked out the death of His Son from long ago. Before time began, the Father chose His Son to become the Savior of His chosen ones. As Jesus went to the cross, He was predetermined for this mission of redemption. Paul wrote, "We speak God's wisdom in a mystery, the hidden wisdom which God predestined before the ages to our glory" (1 Cor. 2:7). This divine wisdom is contained in gospel truth that this world "crucified the Lord of glory" (v. 8). In eternity past, the Father foreordained His Son Jesus Christ to die on the cross in the place of the elect.

GOD IS PRE-ORDAINING

The apostle Peter again used "foreknowledge" inseparably with the sovereign will of the Father in the election of sinners for salvation. He wrote, "Peter, an apostle of Jesus Christ, to those who reside as aliens, scattered throughout Pontus, Galatia, Cappadocia, Asia, and Bithynia, who are chosen according to the foreknowledge of God the Father" (1 Peter 1:1–2). Some wrongly presume that this means God chooses based on those whom He foresees will believe in Jesus. But this word "foreknowledge" is used later in the same chapter: "For He [Jesus Christ] was foreknown before the foundation of the world" (v. 20). In this verse, "foreknown" definitely does *not* mean that God looked down the tunnel of time to see what would happen to the Lord Jesus. This does *not* mean that the Father was forced to adopt the death of His Son as His plan of salvation. Instead, this means that from before time began, the Father chose His Son to be the redeeming Savior of His elect.

Therefore, the meaning of foreknowledge concerning the Father and the Son (v. 20) is exactly what it means regarding the Father and His elect (v. 2). As the Father foreordained Jesus to die on the cross, He likewise foreordained His elect to salvation in Christ. Far from meaning "foresight," this word means the foreordination of those chosen by the Father unto salvation. As the Son was foreknown, so were the elect foreknown.

CHOSEN TO WORSHIP

Contemplating the truth of divine foreknowledge, this means that we were chosen in love by God to worship Him. We love God, quite simply, because He first loved us (1 John 4:19). When we realize that He first set His love on us in eternity past, it humbles us and drives us to our knees in heartfelt devotion to God. The more we understand that He predestined us to the adoption as sons, the more reason we have to give glory to God (Eph. 1:5–6).

This is why when we get to heaven, we will immediately cast our crowns back at the feet of Jesus. In that moment, we will have a far greater realization of the love of God the Father. We will be staggered at the truth that *He* foreknew us, *He* predestined us, *He* called us, *He* justified us, and *He* glorified us. We will cast our crowns before His throne (Rev. 4:10). This will signify our confession that "from Him and through Him and to Him are all things" (Rom. 11:36). This truth of the foreknowledge of God should cause our hearts to be ignited with greater adoration for Him who chose to love us before time began.

Chapter Eighteen

PERFECTLY JUST

The Righteousness of God

*Modern man is betting his eternal destiny there is
no final judgment. That is a tragically fatal mistake.*

—R.C. Sproul

G iven that God is sovereign, it is important that we know that all His dealings are just and fair. Earthly rulers are prone to abuse their authority. Human history reveals that absolute power can corrupt absolutely. Unjust leaders often tip the scales of justice by rewarding evildoers and punishing those who do right. When they have unchecked authority, their administrations can become filled with corruption.

But a charge of injustice can never be brought against God's judicial authority. As the sovereign Lord of the universe, God never acts in our lives or toward others in an unjust manner. He never abuses His authority. In a word, He is righteous—He is completely just. Because of this important attribute, God always does what is right in His dealings with mankind.

The righteousness of God is a necessary aspect of His holiness that causes Him to deal justly with all people. God never misuses His power by violating His own established law. He never rewards those who transgress His ordinances. He never overlooks those who break His statutes. He never disregards those who violate His commandments. On the other hand, He never forgets His people who keep His Word. He remembers those who suffer for doing what is right. In the end, God rewards them for their faithfulness to His Word.

Every one of God's dealings with man is marked by impeccable justice. Every verdict reached in His divine courtroom is the right decision. Every punishment or exoneration is the proper execution of equity. Every acquittal is perfectly pronounced. When the divine gavel comes down, every crime of cosmic treason against Him will be condemned and punished to the fullest extent of the law. Moreover, every good deed done in His name will be fairly and fully rewarded.

The following headings will help us put our arms around this imposing characteristic of God and come to a better understanding of it.

GOD IS JUDGE

To begin this investigation, we want to establish that God—and God *alone*—sits as the moral Judge over the entire universe (1 Sam. 2:10). From His judgment bar, He executes perfect justice over the world (Ps. 96:13; 98:9). The psalmist Asaph writes, "The heavens declare His righteousness, for God Himself is judge" (Ps. 50:6). All the heavenly throng announce the righteousness of God for all creation to hear. With Him, there is never a twisting of right judgment. The scales of His justice never tip unfairly. Again, Asaph states, "God is the Judge; He puts down one and exalts another" (Ps. 75:7). In the end, He always renders His verdicts rightly, exalting one and demoting another as each one deserves.

Regarding the administration of this justice, God has committed all judgment to His Son, Jesus Christ. The Lord Jesus says, "For not even the Father judges anyone, but He has given all judgment to the Son" (John 5:22). The Father has entrusted the weighty responsibility to judge the world into the hands of the Son of God. Jesus adds, "He [the Father] gave Him [the Son] authority to execute judgment, because He is the Son of Man" (v. 27). He claims that not only is He appointed to be the Judge, but He is also given the necessary authority to execute judgment (Matt. 25:31–32). Jesus acknowledges, "All authority has been given to Me in heaven and on earth" (Matt. 28:18). There is no higher court of appeal in the universe—this divine court is *the* supreme court of heaven and earth.

This message of righteous judgment was prevalent in the early church. Peter announced Jesus "is the One who has been appointed by God as Judge of the living and the dead" (Acts 10:42). This day of final judgment is fixed on the divine calendar. Every person has an unbreakable appointment to stand before Jesus Christ on the last day. The apostle Paul confirmed: "He has fixed a day in which He will judge the world in righteousness through a Man whom He has appointed, having furnished proof to all men by raising Him from the dead" (Acts 17:31). This divinely appointed Judge is the Lord Jesus Christ, who will hold court over all mankind (Rev. 20:11–15).

A day of final reckoning also awaits believers. Paul writes,

"For we must all appear before the judgment seat of Christ, so that each one may be recompensed for his deeds in the body, according to what he has done, whether good or bad" (2 Cor. 5:10). This verse is addressed to "we"—all believers. They will be judged not for their sin but for their service. We will each give an account to Christ, as a servant to his Master, for the stewardship of our gifts and opportunities that have been entrusted to us.

GOD IS JUST

In His divine judgments, God is always perfectly just. Abraham asks, "Shall not the Judge of all the earth deal justly?" (Gen. 18:25). This question is, in reality, a strong statement, declaring that God *will* deal justly in every case. The word translated "justly" (Hebrew *mishpat*) means "to render a judgment equitably or fairly." God will always—and only—pass verdicts that are in accordance with His perfect holiness. When God says "eye for eye, tooth for tooth" (Ex. 21:24; cf. Lev. 24:20; Deut. 19:21), He simply means that when justice is to be served, the punishment should fit the crime. So it is likewise carried out by Him.

Moses proclaims that His judicial decisions can never be contrary to justice: "For I proclaim the name of the LORD; ascribe greatness to our God! The Rock! His work is perfect, for all His ways are just; a God of faithfulness and without injustice, righteous and upright is He" (Deut. 32:3–4). This announcement maintains that God always executes perfect justice. He is "without injustice"—a double negative—meaning He will never, *ever* declare an unfair verdict.

There can be no impropriety with God. He always passes His judgments in a perfect manner. He can never be accused of acting with unfairness. In all His deliberations, He always does what is right. He never rewards sinful behavior. He never punishes obedience. God renders righteous justice because He loves what is right. David writes, "He loves righteousness and justice" (Ps. 33:5). He is not morally indifferent in rendering His judgments. Rather, He delights in executing inflexible fairness for all.

The reason God loves righteous judgments is because He Himself is absolutely holy. It is His very nature to love what is right—anything that aligns with His perfect character. God would cease to be holy if He ever rejoiced in injustice. The psalmist writes: "The strength of the King loves justice; You have established equity; You have executed justice and righteousness in Jacob" (Ps. 99:4). God takes delight in carrying out perfect justice in every judicial decision He makes.

All perfect justice belongs to God and proceeds from Him. In fact, the psalmist announces, "Righteousness and justice are the foundation of Your throne" (Ps. 89:14; cf. 97:2). These two divine character qualities—"righteousness and justice"—refer to His strict judgment with which He presides over every life, examining the evidence, rendering the verdict, and executing the sentence. Every judicial decision by God is anchored in unwavering equity.

GOD IS IMPARTIAL

An indispensable part of divine righteousness is the impartiality with which God administers His justice. God plays no favorites in His heavenly courtroom. He does not have one standard for one group, but enforces a different legal code for another. Moses declares, "For the LORD your God is the God of gods and the Lord of lords, the great, the mighty, and the awesome God who does not show partiality nor take a bribe" (Deut. 10:17). God never discriminates in the application of His divine law. His greatness is revealed in the equal treatment under the law He gives to all people.

When King Jehoshaphat was rebuked for the injustice of his reign, he readily repented. The king recognized that if he was to be like God, he had to be fair in His dealings with all people. He confessed, "The LORD our God will have no part in unrighteousness or partiality or the taking of a bribe" (2 Chron. 19:7). Because God is impartial, human government must seek to be the same. When Job accused God of injustice, Elihu responded: "Therefore, listen to me, you men of understanding. Far be it from God to do wickedness, and from the Almighty to do wrong. For He pays a man according to his work, and makes him find it according to his way. Surely, God will not act wickedly, and the Almighty will not pervert justice" (Job 34:10–12). The message was clear—there is no injustice with God, even in Job's great suffering.

This impartiality of God is further taught in the New Testament. Peter says, "I most certainly understand now that God is not one to show partiality" (Acts 10:34). God will treat both Jews and Gentiles alike under the law. The apostle Paul asserts, "For there is no partiality with God" (Rom. 2:11). The word translated "partiality" (Greek *prosōpolempteō*) means "to receive a face." The idea is to give preference to a person or show favoritism because of who he is in his standing in the world (James 2:1–4). Partiality occurs when a verdict is rendered because of an individual's status, influence, or money. Though this can be sadly true in fallen human courts, it is never so with God. A person's standing in his or her community has no bearing on God's judgments toward him.

Paul bluntly writes, "God shows no partiality" (Gal. 2:6). Such unfairness would be impossible with God. "Whatever a man sows, this he will also reap" (Gal. 6:7). God plays no favorites, but administers a one-for-all justice based on His universal standard. Paul further warns that the Lord will discipline the disobedient without any partiality: "For he who does wrong will receive the consequences of the wrong which he has done, and that without partiality" (Col. 3:25).

With straightforward directness, Peter reinforces this same truth regarding God's impartiality: "If you address as Father the One who impartially judges according to each one's work, conduct yourselves in fear during the time of your stay on earth" (1 Peter 1:17). The apostle reminds us that God is keeping detailed records of every person's works. This awareness of God's impartial judgments should stimulate the fear of God in every believer, leading to a desire to serve Him in a manner that pleases Him. Moreover, it should cause us to praise Him (Rev. 19:1–5).

GOD IS REWARDING

Another aspect of the righteousness of God is His dispensing of rewards upon believers. This is called His remunerative justice, by which He rewards His people for their faithful service in His kingdom. The psalmist states, "Men will say, 'Surely there is a reward for the righteous; surely there is a God who judges on earth!'" (Ps. 58:11). Men should know that God judges on the earth and will reward the righteous for their labors in His name (Isa. 40:10). Isaiah says, "Behold His reward is with Him, and His recompense before Him" (Isa. 62:11). Here, God is pictured as holding His reward firmly in hand, ready to give it to those who faithfully carry out His will.

To those who suffer persecution for righteousness, Jesus promises, "Rejoice and be glad, for your reward in heaven is great" (Matt. 5:12). This is meant to encourage believers that they will be fully rewarded in heaven for any physical assaults, verbal insults, or false accusations they have endured in this world for Christ. In the end, God will make right the suffering they have endured for His glory.

On another occasion, Jesus assures believers: "He who receives a prophet in the name of a prophet shall receive a prophet's reward; and he who receives a righteous man in the name of a righteous man shall receive a righteous man's reward. And whoever in the name of a disciple gives to one of these little ones even a cup of cold water to drink, truly I say to you, he shall not lose his reward" (Matt. 10:41–42). This reward is promised for sacrificial service rendered in the name of Christ. Such behind-the-scenes acts of service often go unrecognized by men, but they are remembered by God—and they will be rewarded in the world to come.

The apostle Paul teaches that God will surely reward His faithful ministers: "If any man's work which he has built on it remains, he will receive a reward" (1 Cor. 3:14). This promised reward will come on the last day from the Master Himself. Paul adds that the motives of men's hearts will also be a factor in the final judgment: "Therefore do not go on passing judgment before the time, but wait until the Lord comes who will both bring to light the things hidden in the darkness and disclose the motives of men's hearts; and then each man's praise will come to him from God" (1 Cor. 4:5). God will carefully appraise not only what a believer does but *why* he did it (1 Cor. 9:17).

Paul again writes: "Whatever you do, do your work heartily,

as for the Lord rather than for men, knowing that from the Lord you will receive the reward of the inheritance. It is the Lord Christ whom you serve" (Col. 3:23–24). Since believers ultimately serve Christ, not men, it is the Lord whom they should strive to honor.

The author of Hebrews assures us that God will not forget any good work performed in His name: "For God is not unjust so as to forget your work and the love which you have shown toward His name, in having ministered and in still ministering to the saints" (Heb. 6:10). This truth about the righteousness of God enabled Moses to consider "the reproach of Christ greater riches than the treasures of Egypt; for he was looking to the reward" (Heb. 11:26). Even so, every believer should be "looking to the reward."

The apostle Peter concurs: "But even if you should suffer for the sake of righteousness, you are blessed. And do not fear their intimidation, and do not be troubled" (1 Peter 3:14). The persecution of the world will usher in the promised blessing of God. "If you are reviled for the name of Christ, you are blessed, because the Spirit of glory and of God rests on you" (1 Peter 4:14). The entire sweeping narrative of the Bible concludes with the climactic promise that Jesus Christ is returning and will reward His saints: "Behold, I am coming quickly, and My reward is with Me, to render to every man according to what he has done" (Rev. 22:12). When Jesus comes again, He will repay His people for their faithfulness to Him. Such hope should be a powerful motivation to persevere "under trial" in doing what is right (James 1:12).

GOD IS AVENGING

The antithesis of divine remuneration is God's avenging of the mistreatment inflicted by evildoers on His people. God says,

"Vengeance is Mine, and retribution" (Deut. 32:35). While He rewards the persecution endured by His people, God will make right the evil injustices committed against them by inflicting vengeance upon the wicked. The psalmist says, "O LORD, God of vengeance, God of vengeance, shine forth!" (Ps. 94:1). This avenging of wrong suffered may not occur during this lifetime. But to be sure, it will be fully delivered in the world to come. The psalmist sings God's praises for overthrowing his enemies: "'Many times they have persecuted me from my youth up,' let Israel now say, 'many times they have persecuted me from my youth up; yet they have not prevailed against me. The plowers plowed upon my back; they lengthened their furrows.' The LORD is righteous; He has cut in two the cords of the wicked" (Ps. 129:1–4). God will surely avenge the ill treatment His people have suffered at the hands of the wicked.

When the apostle John was taken up into heaven and given the divine perspective on the world scene, he saw "underneath the altar the souls of those who had been slain because of the word of God, and because of the testimony which they had maintained" (Rev. 6:9). They cry out with a loud voice, "How long, O Lord, holy and true, will You refrain from judging and avenging our blood on those who dwell on the earth?" (v. 10). "They were told that they should rest for a little while longer, until the number of their fellow servants and their brethren who were to be killed even as they had been, would be completed also" (v. 11). God will surely avenge the bloodshed of martyrs. In His sovereign justice, He will unleash unprecedented affliction upon their persecutors.

At the end of this age, God will inflict His wrath upon evil men who have put to death His saints (Rev. 16:5–6). John records,

"Hallelujah! Salvation and glory and power belong to our God; because His judgments are true and righteous; for He has judged the great harlot who was corrupting the earth with her immorality, and He has avenged the blood of His bond-servants on her" (Rev. 19:1–2). The just retribution of God will be inflicted on the wicked who harm believers. Be assured that God will settle all accounts in the end.

GOD IS PUNISHING

As a righteous God, He also administers punishment on law-breaking sinners for their rebellious disobedience to divine law. This aspect of divine righteousness is known as His punitive justice. God cannot make a law and establish a penalty, but fail to execute the punishment when that law is violated. When the divine commandment is broken, His solemn punishment must be meted out. Otherwise, God would be unjust and no longer be a holy judge.

This principle of punitive justice was first pronounced in the garden. God said to Adam and Eve, "From any tree of the garden you may eat freely; but from the tree of the knowledge of good and evil you shall not eat, for in the day that you eat from it you will surely die" (Gen. 2:16–17). When this divine commandment was broken, God rightly delivered His punishment on them— death. The result was that "the LORD God sent him out from the garden of Eden" (Gen. 3:23). By this punishment, they suffered the just penalty under the divine curse. They immediately died spiritually, and they would ultimately die physically as well.

This inevitable consequence of death for disobedience against God's law has been reinforced throughout the centuries. According to Moses, God "repays those who hate Him to their faces, to destroy them; He will not delay with him who hates Him, He will repay him to his face" (Deut. 7:10). Any crime committed against the high court of heaven merits spiritual death.

Solomon stresses that the wicked will not escape the just punishment of God: "Assuredly, the evil man will not go unpunished" (Prov. 11:21). Likewise, the prophet Isaiah records that God will render judgment upon all the rebellious nations: "According to their deeds, so He will repay, wrath to His adversaries, recompense to His enemies; to the coastlands He will make recompense" (Isa. 59:18). This judgment would come not only upon unbelieving Gentiles in pagan nations, but upon the unconverted in Israel (Isa. 63:1–3). The message is clear that God plays no favorites in dispensing His punishing justice.

In the days of Israel's apostasy, God said: "Behold, all souls are Mine; the soul of the father as well as the soul of the son is Mine. The soul who sins will die" (Ezek. 18:4). The promised punishment of cosmic treason against God results in physical death. For those who remained unconverted, it leads to their eternal death. The prophet Nahum asserted the same severe punishment on wicked Nineveh: "A jealous and avenging God is the LORD; the LORD is avenging and wrathful. The LORD takes vengeance on His adversaries, and He reserves wrath for His enemies" (Nah. 1:2). Holy and just, God must punish sin to the fullest extent of His law.

This truth of punitive justice remained true in the New Testament. The apostle Paul confirmed, "The wages of sin is death" (Rom. 6:23). Sin always results in death. In the first warning passage in Hebrews, its author wrote, "For if the word spoken through angels proved unalterable, and every transgression and disobedience received a just penalty, how will we escape if we neglect so great a salvation?" (Heb. 2:2–3). He again warned, "How much severer punishment do you think he will deserve who has trampled under foot the Son of God, and has regarded as unclean the blood of the covenant by which he was sanctified, and has insulted the Spirit of grace?" (Heb. 10:29). James reinforced, "Then when lust has conceived, it gives birth to sin; and when sin is accomplished, it brings forth death" (James 1:15). The punitive result of all sin is the justly deserved death penalty.

GOD IS JUSTIFIER

Because He is the perfectly righteous God, He alone can meet the demands of His own law. Only God is able to provide the perfect righteousness required for sinners to find the just acceptance they need in His sight. This required righteousness is given by God Himself in the forensic act of justification. Through this legal transaction, God is both "just and the justifier of the one who has faith in Jesus" (Rom. 3:26). God is perfectly "just" in that He administers perfect justice for sin in the death of His Son. If He is to receive His elect, they must be declared righteous. Thus, God is the "justifier" of the unrighteous when He imputes the perfect righteousness of Jesus Christ to the one who believes in Him (Rom. 8:33–34).

This crucial point is the very heart of the gospel. The apostle Paul writes, "For in it the righteousness of God is revealed from faith for faith; as it is written, 'But the righteous man shall live by faith'" (Rom. 1:17). This righteousness that comes from God is received on the basis of faith alone (Rom. 4:3, 5). To the one who believes in Jesus Christ, God credits His righteousness (Phil. 3:9). Again, Paul states: "But now apart from the Law the righteousness of God has been manifested, being witnessed by the Law and the Prophets, even the righteousness of God through faith in Jesus Christ for all those who believe; for there is no distinction" (Rom. 3:21–22). This divine righteousness is promised in the free offer of the gospel.

Paul explains how this righteousness was secured: "He made Him who knew no sin to be sin on our behalf, so that we might become the righteousness of God in Him" (2 Cor. 5:21). Here is the astonishing double exchange at the cross. All the sins of all who would believe in Christ were laid on Him. At the same time, the "righteousness of God" is imputed or credited to those who believe in Jesus Christ. Jesus Christ Himself obtained this perfect righteousness by His sinless life and substitutionary death. Herein He secured the perfect righteousness necessary to be credited to believers (Gal. 2:16).

In His incarnation, Jesus Christ entered this world both to live and die in our place. Paul teaches, "But when the fullness of the time came, God sent forth His Son, born of a woman, born under the Law, so that He might redeem those who were under the Law, that we might receive the adoption as sons" (Gal. 4:4–5). We have all disobeyed the law, incurring its punishment. But Jesus was born "under the Law," meaning He assumed our place of direct accountability to obey the divine law. Throughout His earthly life, Jesus perfectly obeyed the law in our place. His obedience was "to fulfill all righteousness" (Matt. 3:15) on our behalf. Those who trust Him are dressed in His righteousness, obtained by His obedience under the law.

ARE YOU READY?

The day is coming when every person will stand before Jesus Christ and give an account of his thoughts, motives, and actions. This appointed time is looming on the horizon of time and is fast approaching. It is altogether unavoidable. Are you ready to face the tribunal of heaven? If you are an unbeliever, you need to settle this matter out of court. You need someone to represent you before the Judge and plead your case. You need someone with a right standing under the law to defend you. That One is—and must be—Jesus Christ.

The apostle John writes, "If anyone sins, we have an Advocate with the Father, Jesus Christ the righteous; and He Himself is the propitiation for our sins; and not for ours only, but also for those of the whole world" (1 John 2:1–2). God has appointed His Son, Jesus Christ, to be the Advocate of sinners. He acts like a defense attorney who pleads His own merit on behalf of those who place their faith in Him. Jesus is the only One who can clear you of all charges brought against you. For each believer, Jesus gains an acquittal for all charges brought against them.

You must believe upon Him, and receive the glorious benefits of this divine execution of God's righteousness. Truly, "Therefore there is now no condemnation for those who are in Christ Jesus" (Rom. 8:1).

Chapter Nineteen

PROFOUNDLY ANGRY

The Wrath of God

As God's mercies are new every morning toward His people,
so His anger is new every morning against the wicked.

—MATTHEW HENRY

As we come to the last attribute of God that we will consider, we recognize it is by no means the least important. In fact, everything in this study has been building to this climactic ending. This divine attribute is critically important for any right understanding of who God is. I am referring to the wrath of God. This trait has not been saved until now because it brings up a provocative subject. We must make no apology for any truth about God—especially with the truth of divine wrath.

In our study, this vital attribute of God comes last because it has been necessary that we lay a firm foundation with the other aspects of His nature. We are now ready to address this intensive truth about the character of God. Some people speak of the wrath of God apologetically, as if it is the dark side of God. But the Bible says, "God is Light, and in Him there is no darkness at all" (1 John 1:5). Let us be clear—there is *no* dark side of God. He is *all* light. Every attribute of God is absolutely pure and full of light, and this includes the wrath of God.

The holiness of God demands that He be angered by sin. Divine wrath is the necessary response of His moral purity toward whoever and whatever breaks His law. God is flawless, without any moral defect, and He must be full of holy wrath toward all sin. He cannot be indifferent toward any iniquity. God possesses an intense indignation against all that is unholy. This is true not only against sin, but also against the sinner. Divine wrath must be enraged against all that does not conform to His moral perfection. Otherwise, God would cease to be infinitely holy.

The apostle Paul writes, "For the wrath of God is revealed from heaven against all ungodliness and unrighteousness of men who suppress the truth in unrighteousness" (Rom. 1:18). The word "wrath" (Greek *orgē*) represents the enflamed anger of God toward the sinfulness of humanity. This Greek word comes into the English language as "orgy," describing the heated, carnal lusts of lewd, immoral parties. The overarching idea this word captures is the intense "heavy breathing" response of holy God against the sinfulness of man. God is enkindled by His burning passion against whatever does not conform to His own perfect holiness.

Paul stresses the same: "But because of your stubbornness and unrepentant heart you are storing up wrath for yourself in the day of wrath and revelation of the righteous judgment of God" (Rom. 2:5). The "day of wrath" is a reference to the last day, when God will settle His accounts. The unconverted are amassing wrath upon wrath that will be finally unleashed by God. In that day, they will be overwhelmed by a torrential deluge of divine anger against them. Because God is perfectly good, it is crucial that He punish wrongdoing in eternal hell. Divine wrath is the necessary counterpart to perfect holiness.

We proceed soberly in considering this truth, knowing what a solemn aspect of the character of God this is. To best organize our thoughts, the following categories of wrath will help us think accurately about this divine attribute.

GOD IS PROVOKED

As a place to begin, God is presently angry with sinners in their sin. He is never indifferent toward iniquity, but is provoked deeply by it. Moses addressed the nation of Israel, saying: "Then the LORD heard the sound of your words, and He was angry and took an oath, saying, 'Not one of these men, this evil generation, shall see the good land which I swore to give your fathers'" (Deut. 1:34–35). The word translated "angry" (Hebrew *qatsaf*) means "to provoke to wrath or anger, to put oneself in a rage." This passage reveals the zealous anger of the holy God toward transgressors who are rebellious against Him.

In a later sermon, Moses proclaims: "Remember, do not forget how you provoked [*qatsaf*] the LORD your God to wrath in the wilderness; from the day that you left the land of Egypt until you arrived at this place, you have been rebellious against the LORD. Even at Horeb you provoked [*qatsaf*] the LORD to wrath, and the LORD was so angry with you that He would have destroyed you" (Deut. 9:7–8). In no uncertain terms, Moses states how the sins of God's people "provoked" (*qatsaf*) His wrath. Far from being nonchalant toward their sin, God was kindled in His anger by their rebellion. This wickedness did not cause God to be altered in His being. Rather, He remained the same as He always was in His holy hatred of sin.

Joshua announced the same warning to the new generation that entered the promised land. He declared that God was incensed in His anger with their sin. He says, "If you rebel against the LORD today, He will be angry with the whole congregation of Israel tomorrow" (Josh. 22:18). "Angry" (*qatsaf*) is the same Hebrew word that was translated earlier as "provoked" in Deuteronomy 1:34 and 9:7. Here, we see that God has a self-determined anger against that which is unholy and contrary to His flawless nature.

Other passages reinforce this truth. The psalmist writes, "They also provoked [*qatsaf*] Him to wrath at the waters of Meribah" (Ps. 106:32). Zechariah records, "For thus says the LORD of hosts, 'Just as I purposed to do harm to you when your fathers provoked [*qatsaf*] Me to wrath,' says the LORD of hosts" (Zech. 8:14). In each of these texts, God demonstrates how He was moved to wrath by the sins of the people. In this very moment, this same wrath of God is provoked against sinners and their sin.

GOD IS FIERY

The Bible teaches that God is ignited with fiery anger toward sin and the sinner. "Then the anger of the LORD burned against Moses" (Ex. 4:14). The "burning" (Hebrew *harah*) of God's "anger" (Hebrew *af*) literally means "the burning of the nose." This portrays someone breathing out of their nose with intense fury. In this case, it is the burning anger of God being released, as if, metaphorically, it is being snorted out of His nostrils. The imagery is that God is enraged, as if billowing smoke is spewing out of His nose. God is pictured like a charging bull, breathing out heated fury, ready to charge the sinner who angers Him. That is how God acted toward Moses at his hesitation to obey His will. Likewise, He was filled with a burning anger against Israel when they worshiped other gods (Num. 25:3).

Moses sang about this divine wrath after He drowned Pharaoh's army in the Red Sea: "At the blast of Your nostrils the waters were piled up" (Ex. 15:8). In that momentous day, the boiling hot wrath of God consumed the Egyptians, immediately sending them to His greater wrath in hellfire below. Again, God says, "My anger [*af*] will be kindled, and I will kill you with the sword, and your wives shall become widows and your children fatherless" (Ex. 22:24). In this verse, the wrath of God is pictured as a blazing furnace—a fiery inferno—that will justly consume sinners.

In the wilderness, God's anger boiled over against those who complained against Him: "Now the people became like those who complain of adversity in the hearing of the LORD; and when the LORD heard it, His anger [*af*] was kindled, and the fire of the LORD burned among them and consumed some of the outskirts of the camp" (Num. 11:1). The wrath of the Lord burned with intense outrage because of their sins committed against Him. Again, "Moses heard the people weeping throughout their families, each man at the doorway of his tent; and the anger [*af*] of the LORD was kindled greatly" (v. 10). To be sure, God is never morally neutral against sinners but is full of righteous fury.

God warned His people that when they entered the promised land, the Canaanites would tempt them with false gods. When this occurred, God said it would enrage His anger: "For they will turn your sons away from following Me to serve other gods; then the anger [*af*] of the LORD will be kindled against you and He will quickly destroy you" (Deut. 7:4). God is not indifferent toward this grievous offense. Like a burning fire, God's anger would be "kindled" and would destroy the disobedient unless they repented.

The anger of God is always aroused whenever the wicked rebel against Him. The psalmist writes, "Then He will speak to them in His anger [*af*] and terrify them in His fury" (Ps. 2:5). This is the holy outrage of God against the rebellious global conspiracy against Him. He burns with anger when sinners shake their defiant fists in His face. After God's threats of judgment, the psalmist urges sinners to repent while there is time: "Do homage to the Son, that He not become angry [*anef*], and you perish in the way, for His wrath may soon be kindled" (v. 12). "Be angry" (Hebrew *anef*) means "to breathe hard" as an expression of anger. If they do not humble themselves before the Son of God, this divine anger will soon be ignited. If they do not turn to the Son *now*, it will be too late to escape the smoldering fire of His glowing hot wrath.

The psalmist trembled before God because of His righteous anger: "You, even You, are to be feared; and who may stand in Your presence when once You are angry [*af*]?" (Ps. 76:7). He knew that none can stand before Him when He is angered. God Himself says, "For forty years I loathed that generation, and said they are a people who err in their heart, and they do not know My ways. Therefore I swore in My anger [*af*], truly they shall not enter into My rest" (Ps. 95:10–11; cf. Heb. 3:10–11). Ultimately, this divine anger was realized against this generation.

GOD IS FURIOUS

Another description of smoldering wrath is the infinite fury of God against sin. The psalmist writes, "You withdrew all Your fury [*evrah*]; You turned away from Your burning anger" (Ps. 85:3). The word translated "fury" (Hebrew *evrah*) means "outpouring, overflow, excess." This indicates the overflowing rage of God against His sinful people, before the rising tide of His anger was turned away from them. This same word is used elsewhere: "He sent upon them His burning anger, fury [*evrah*] and indignation and trouble, a band of destroying angels" (Ps. 78:49). In this verse, the anger of God against sinners is joined with His fury— an overwhelming storm of divine anger, fury, and indignation. Moses writes: "For all our days have declined in Your fury [*evrah*]; we have finished our years like a sigh. . . . Who understands the power of Your anger and Your fury [*evrah*], according to the fear that is due You?" (Ps. 90:9, 11). The fury of God is so great against sin that its infinite force is incomprehensible to human understanding. The full extent of the fury of God is inconceivable in its greatness.

In the final day of wrath, God will unleash His fury: "By the fury [*evrah*] of the LORD of hosts the land is burned up, and the people are like fuel for the fire" (Isa. 9:19). This describes God's heated anger against the arrogance of His people. Isaiah warns, "Behold, the day of the LORD is coming, cruel, with fury [*evrah*] and burning anger, to make the land a desolation; and He will exterminate its sinners from it" (Isa. 13:9). God says, "Therefore I will make the heavens tremble, and the earth will be shaken from its place at the fury of the LORD of hosts in the day of His burning anger" (v. 13). In Isaiah, this outpouring of divine fury anticipated the final destruction of the sinful Babylonian Empire. Likewise, Jeremiah writes about the destruction of God's own city, Jerusalem: "The Lord has swallowed up; He has not spared all the habitations of Jacob. In His wrath [*evrah*] He has thrown down the strongholds of the daughter of Judah; He has brought them down to the ground; He has profaned the kingdom and its princes" (Lam. 2:2). The wrath of God literally overflows from His holy character like rushing waters after a dam break.

God emphatically says, "I will pour out My indignation on you; I will blow on you with the fire of My wrath [*evrah*], and I will give you into the hand of brutal men, skilled in destruction" (Ezek. 21:31). In His wrath, this outpouring of divine fury will torch and consume sinners. Again, God warns, "I will gather you and blow on you with the fire of My wrath [*evrah*], and you will be melted in the midst of it" (Ezek. 22:21). The fire of divine wrath will be utterly unbearable in that day as sinners will be melted down. "In My zeal and in My blazing wrath [*evrah*] I declare that on that day there will surely be a great earthquake in the land of Israel" (Ezek. 38:19). Here, God promises His furious wrath will be unleashed with "zeal" (*qinah*)—that is, with the intense outburst of His anger.

GOD IS INDIGNANT

A further aspect of divine wrath is His indignation toward the manifold sin of mankind. The psalmist David writes, "God is a righteous judge, and a God who has indignation every day" (Ps. 7:11). "Indignation" (Hebrew *zaam*) means "to be angrily indignant, to denounce." This indignation fills God *every day*—not just on the last day—toward the wicked. It is poised and ready to be unleashed in this present day. In the next verses, God is pictured as a divine warrior, as One who fights against His enemies. David explains, "If a man does not repent, He will sharpen His sword; He has bent His bow and made it ready. He has also prepared for Himself deadly weapons; He makes His arrows fiery shafts" (vv. 12–13). God is pictured with the arrows of His wrath already placed in the bow of His indignation. They are aimed at the sinner, ready to be released, and will pierce the soul and inflict eternal destruction.

Isaiah writes, "He [God] will be indignant [*zaam*] toward His enemies. For behold, the LORD will come in fire and His chariots like the whirlwind, to render His anger with fury, and His rebuke with flames of fire" (Isa. 66:14–15). In that awful day, God will burn with indignation like a blazing inferno that will consume His adversaries. God later says, "They may build, but I will tear down; and men will call them the wicked territory, and the people toward whom the LORD is indignant [*zaam*] forever" (Mal. 1:4). There will be no quenching the fiery indignation of God against the wicked, unless they repent.

In the New Testament, the apostle Paul again addresses this divine indignation against sinners. Those who "do not obey the truth, but obey unrighteousness" will receive "wrath and indignation" (Rom. 2:8). "Indignation" (Greek *thymos*) means "hot anger, passion." It represents the vehement anger of God that results in His relentless outburst of wrath. The root meaning of *thymos* is related to "something moving rapidly." It was used of someone swiftly pursuing an enemy to inflict harm upon them. On the final day of judgment, God will rapidly pursue and suddenly overtake rebellious sinners who are running away from Him.

His indignation will be like an erupting volcano, spewing divine wrath, from which the unrepentant cannot escape. In the end, they will be eternally consumed.

In other verses, this same word *thymos* is translated "wrath." The apostle John writes that in hell, unbelievers "will drink of the wine of the wrath [*thymos*] of God, which is mixed in full strength in the cup of His anger" (Rev. 14:10). Fully fermented wrath, in its most robust potency, will be served to damned souls. Likewise, we read, "The angel swung his sickle to the earth and gathered the clusters from the vine of the earth, and threw them into the great wine press of the wrath [*thymos*] of God" (v. 19). This divine "wrath" (*thymos*) is what will fill that cup of His heated indignation that will be served in hell. There, unbelievers will drink from this cup without end. In this place of horror, they will consume God's wrath and be consumed by it—forever.

When Jesus Christ comes, John records, "From His mouth comes a sharp sword, so that with it He may strike down the nations, and He will rule them with a rod of iron; and He treads the wine press of the fierce wrath [*thymos*] of God, the Almighty" (Rev. 19:15). This imagery portrays God's wrath with the same crushing power as the ancient practice of stomping grapes underfoot with the heel in order to produce wine. He will crush His adversaries, and their blood will be splattered like grape juice. The outburst of divine indignation in that day will eternally torment those who have rejected Him.

GOD IS ABHORRING

The wrath of God also causes Him to abhor those who rebel against Him. The psalmist writes, "For they provoked Him with their high places and aroused His jealousy with their graven images. When God heard, He was filled with wrath and greatly abhorred Israel" (Ps. 78:58–59). The word translated "abhorred" (Hebrew *maas*) means "to hate, to despise, to reject, to cast away." There is an intense loathing that God has for those who worship false gods. Another psalmist writes, "But You have cast off and rejected [*maas*], You have been full of wrath against Your anointed" (Ps. 89:38). Here, the Hebrew word *maas* is translated "rejected." God says He utterly rejects with contempt those who "forsake My law" and "violate My statutes" (vv. 30–31).

The psalmist quotes God as saying, "For forty years I loathed that generation" (Ps. 95:10). "Loathed" (Hebrew *qut*) means "to detest." For four long decades, God was angry with this entire generation that so blatantly rebelled against Him.

GOD IS HATING

The Hebrew word *sane* is used synonymously with the abhorrence and indignation of God. It refers to the divine hate He has for the unrighteous. This is His intense hatred of the unregenerate sinner in his sin. David says: "You hate [*sane*] all who do iniquity. You destroy those who speak falsehood; the LORD abhors the man of bloodshed and deceit" (Ps. 5:5–6). This strong word "hate" (*sane*) means "to find repugnant, to utterly reject." Because God is perfectly holy, He must react against and reject all sin. Moreover, He must also abhor "the man of bloodshed" who commits sin. God will eternally "destroy" the sinner as the object of His wrath.

David reinforces this formidable reality of God's hatred toward the unrighteous: "The LORD tests the righteous and the wicked, and the one who loves violence His soul hates [*sane*]. Upon the wicked He will rain snares; fire and brimstone and burning wind will be the portion of their cup" (Ps. 11:5–6). "Hates" (*sane*) sometimes means not to love (Gen. 29:31, 33; Deut. 21:15). But more often, it means to be strongly hated. The word describes how Joseph's brothers "hated" him and sold him into slavery (Gen. 37:4–5, 8). By this, we learn that the wrath of God is fueled by a holy abhorrence of sinners.

The psalmist gives a prophetic messianic description of the Lord's anointed: "You have loved righteousness and hated [*sane*] wickedness" (Ps. 45:7; cf. Heb. 1:9). Never casual about sin, the Messiah aggressively hates all wickedness. His love of holiness necessitates that He hate unholiness. Otherwise, He would be a self-contradiction. Solomon writes, "There are six things which the LORD hates [*sane*], yes, seven which are an abomination to Him" (Prov. 6:16). Simply put, holy God hates any manifestation of unholiness.

Religious hypocrisy in worship arouses the hatred of God. God Himself says: "I hate [*sane*] your new moon festivals and your appointed feasts, they have become a burden to Me; I am weary of bearing them" (Isa. 1:14). This is the love-hate relationship God has in the worship of His name. "For I, the LORD, love justice, I hate [*sane*] robbery in the burnt offering" (Isa. 61:8). "My inheritance [Israel] has become to Me like a lion in the forest; she has roared against Me; therefore I have come to hate [*sane*] her" (Jer. 12:8). Far from being indifferent, God hates those who roar with defiant arrogance against Him.

Further evidence of this is seen when God says, "I sent you all My servants the prophets, again and again, saying, 'Oh, do not do this abominable thing which I hate [*sane*]'" (Jer. 44:4). Without any attempt to conceal this hatred, God says, "I hate [*sane*], I reject your festivals, nor do I delight in your solemn assemblies" (Amos 5:21). Because of Israel's blatant duplicity in worship, they were abhorrent in the sight of God.

GOD IS VENGEFUL

The wrath of God further includes His vengeance upon those who break His law and offend His holiness. To those who rebel, God says, "I will also bring upon you a sword which will execute vengeance" (Lev. 26:25). "Vengeance" (Hebrew *naqam*) indicates God's intense anger against His enemies that inflicts punishment for the offense inflicted against Him. God says He will repay sinners for their wickedness: "Vengeance [*naqam*] is Mine, and retribution, in due time their foot will slip; for the day of their calamity is near" (Deut. 32:35). As the Lawgiver, God must execute the due penalty when His law is broken. Otherwise, He would be an unfit Judge. Disobedience to the divine moral code always demands full retribution by God, which is death (Gen. 2:17; 2 Kings 14:6; Jer. 31:30; Ezek. 18:4, 20).

In the New Testament, "vengeance" (Greek *ekdikēsis*) means the punishing retribution administered in carrying out justice. It conveys God's avenging of what is wrong. It is a compound word, combining *ek*, meaning "out of," with *dikēsis*, meaning "righteousness of justice." The word refers to the execution of God's righteous judgment that proceeds out from Himself. It is the inflicting of a just punishment on the person who commits an offense against God. Vengeance is the necessary response of holy God against sinners. It is when God rightly avenges the wrong suffered against Him.

Paul writes, "Leave room for the wrath of God, for it is written, 'Vengeance [*ekdikēsis*] is Mine, I will repay,' says the Lord" (Rom. 12:19). At the end of this age, Jesus Christ will be "dealing out retribution [*ekdikēsis*] to those who do not know God and to those who do not obey the gospel of our Lord Jesus" (2 Thess. 1:8). Jesus will settle His accounts with full retribution in the end. The writer of Hebrews reinforces the same: "Every transgression and disobedience" will receive "a just penalty" (Heb. 2:2). Further, he records, "For we know Him who said, 'Vengeance [*ekdikēsis*] is Mine, I will repay.' And again, 'The Lord will judge His people.' It is a terrifying thing to fall into the hands of the living God" (Heb. 10:30–31). Again, "vengeance" means the injured party is vindicated by punishing the offender. In the analogy, God is the offended party who must punish the offending sinner.

THE ONLY HOPE OF ESCAPE

There is no humanly devised way to escape this escalating wrath of God on sin. The only hope for deliverance from its eternal destruction is found in a singular person. Only through personal faith in Jesus Christ can sinners be shielded from God's wrath on that fateful day. On the cross, He suffered the wrath of God for the sin of all who would turn to Him in repentance. As Jesus bore our sins on the cross, He likewise suffered the vengeance of God that was due to rebellious lawbreakers. Christ received the full measure of divine wrath so that He would propitiate—or appease—the righteous anger of God (Heb. 2:17).

The apostle Paul explains, "God displayed [Jesus] publicly as a propitiation in His blood" (Rom. 3:25). The word "propitiation" (Greek *hilastērion*) means "appeasement or satisfaction."

The death of Jesus Christ placated the wrath of God against those for whom Christ died. His substitutionary death propitiated the anger of God toward sinners who believe in Him. There is now "peace with God through our Lord Jesus Christ" (Rom. 5:1).

The apostle John writes, "Jesus Christ the righteous . . . is the propitiation for our sins; and not for ours only, but also for those of the whole world" (1 John 2:1–2). That is to say, Jesus Christ, on the cross, satisfied the righteous demands of God by absorbing the just wrath that was due to fall on guilty sinners.

Have you believed on Jesus Christ? He is offered to you as the only Savior from the wrath to come. "How will we escape if we neglect so great a salvation?" (Heb. 2:3). Come by faith to Christ, and He will save you forever.

Chapter Twenty

EXCEEDINGLY WORTHY

The Worship of God

Be not afraid of saying too much in the praises of God;
all the danger is of saying too little.

—MATTHEW HENRY

We began our survey of the attributes of God by examining a dramatic encounter that Moses had with the living God. This leader of the exodus asked God, "Show me Your glory!" (Ex. 33:18). God chose to answer this daring request affirmatively. At first, God responded by manifesting Himself as a bright, shining light, so blinding that Moses had to hide behind a rock to shield his eyes. Then God descended in a shekinah glory cloud and preached His name and nature to Moses (34:1–9). This was an amazing display of divine glory—far more than Moses had yet experienced or could have ever imagined.

The effect of the greater revelation of God given to Moses was overwhelming. It crushed him in the depth of his being and was heavier than he could bear. Under this weight of glory, he immediately fell to the ground and bowed before God. In response to such majesty, he could not humble himself enough. In this moment, Moses "worshiped" God (34:8). The word translated "worship" (Hebrew *shachah*) means "to bow down." He lowered himself in the presence of God in an act of utter homage. He subordinated himself before One who had shown Himself to be infinitely his superior.

We have observed many different features of the glorious character of God—like the different facets on a beautifully cut diamond. There is still more of the divine nature to consider than what we could possibly address in one volume like this. We could spend the rest of our lives studying the being of God, and even then, we would only begin to scratch the surface of who He is. Infinite God far exceeds our finite minds. We have nevertheless examined some of the basic parameters of the greatness of this God. Though we have not encompassed the whole subject of God—such would be impossible—we have learned many truths of what He has revealed about Himself.

As Moses humbled himself in awestruck worship of God, so must we. Such self-effacement is always necessary in any pure worship of God. No true worshiper can stand proudly in the presence of this awesome God. The more we learn about God, the more we should love and adore Him—and lower ourselves in humility before Him. As a result of the riches of our study, the following should encourage us in this pursuit to know Him more deeply.

GOD IS APPROACHABLE

Though God "dwells in unapproachable light" (1 Tim. 6:16), He has provided the avenue—the *only* way—through which we unworthy sinners may approach Him. This exclusive access is given through the Lord Jesus Christ. God the Father sent His only begotten Son into this world to provide the one way to come into His presence and find acceptance with Him. The writer of Hebrews states, "We have confidence to enter the holy place by the blood of Jesus, by a new and living way which He inaugurated for us through the veil, that is, His flesh" (Heb. 10:19–20). Jesus pioneered this way to God—*He* is the way.

This means to approach God was designed by the Father Himself and executed by the Son through His sacrificial death on the cross. The writer of Hebrews urges us, "Let us draw near with a sincere heart in full assurance of faith, having our hearts sprinkled clean from an evil conscience and our bodies washed with pure water" (Heb. 10:22). Only those who have been washed in the precious blood of Christ may find forgiveness and enter the presence of holy God (Heb. 9:22). The blood of Jesus is able to cleanse the vilest offender and present him faultless before the throne of God with full acceptance (1 John 1:7, 9).

Without any equivocation, Jesus says, "I am the way, and the truth, and the life; no one comes to the Father but through Me" (John 14:6). Christ announces that He opens up the only way to God the Father. Otherwise, we would have no access to Him. Apart from Jesus, we would be barred from the presence of God. But through Jesus, we may boldly approach the Father with full confidence. "Therefore let us draw near with confidence to the throne of grace, so that we may receive mercy and find grace to help in time of need" (Heb. 4:16). When we come in the name of Jesus, we find full acceptance with God. Through this great salvation, we have been granted unlimited access to God in worship, fellowship, and prayer.

By His sin-bearing death, Jesus has removed the barrier of our transgressions that prevented us from coming to the Father. The apostle Paul states, "Through Him [Jesus Christ] we both [Jews and Gentiles] have our access in one Spirit to the Father" (Eph. 2:18). Jesus is our sole passage to the Father. Paul further says that in Christ, God has "canceled out the certificate of debt consisting of decrees against us, which was hostile to us; and He has taken it out of the way, having nailed it to the cross" (Col. 2:14). By His death, Jesus removed the otherwise insurmountable barrier of the penalty of our sins. For all time, He took our sins "out of the way" that had previously prohibited our access to God. He has opened up the one and only entrance to the Father.

This previously unapproachable God is now approachable through the merit of Jesus Christ. The gates of paradise have been swung wide open. In fact, God invites us to join Him, through the gospel. Jesus Himself calls us to come to Himself. He says, "If anyone is thirsty, let him come to Me and drink" (John 7:37). He bids us come: "Come to Me, all who are weary and heavy-laden, and I will give you rest" (Matt. 11:28). The invitation is clear—you must *come*.

GOD IS KNOWABLE

When we come to God by faith in Christ, we enter into the personal knowledge of the Father. Jesus says, "This is eternal life, that they may know You, the only true God, and Jesus Christ whom You have sent" (John 17:3). Christianity, unlike other religions, is not concerned with external matters of outward rituals and superficial routines. Instead, it is rooted in a living relationship with God in the heart. To know God is to enjoy the experiential knowledge of Him in the depth of the soul. This means we may no longer merely know *about* Him, but actually know Him. It is to love Him as you would another person. The only difference is that this relationship is much closer and far more intimate, because the Spirit of God dwells inside of us who believe.

Concerning the priority of knowing God, Jeremiah records, "Thus says the LORD, 'Let not a wise man boast of his wisdom, and let not the mighty man boast of his might, let not a rich man boast of his riches; but let him who boasts boast of this, that he understands and knows Me, that I am the LORD who exercises lovingkindness, justice and righteousness on earth; for I delight in these things,' declares the LORD" (Jer. 9:23–24). God declares that the greatest thing in all the world is to know Him. This relationship is far greater than attaining worldly power, accumulating riches, or acquiring knowledge.

We come to know God when we believe on His Son. Jesus says the only people who know the Father are those "to whom the Son wills to reveal Him" (Matt. 11:27). When we entrust our souls to Christ, He immediately ushers us into union and communion with the Father. Jesus Christ, as it were, takes us by the hand, leads us to God the Father, and introduces us to Him as His newly adopted child—though the Father has foreknown us from eternity past.

Once Paul came to know Christ, the goal of his life was to know Him deeper and more intimately. He wrote, "More than that, I count all things to be loss in view of the surpassing value of knowing Christ Jesus my Lord, for whom I have suffered the loss of all things, and count them but rubbish so that I may gain Christ" (Phil. 3:8). Peter said the same, that we may "grow in the grace and knowledge of our Lord and Savior Jesus Christ" (2 Peter 3:18).

For Paul, it was worth the loss of everything that he once held dear in order to gain the surpassing knowledge of Christ. Once he knew Christ, he longed to know Him yet more: "That I may know Him and the power of His resurrection and the fellowship of His sufferings, being conformed to His death" (Phil. 3:10). Whatever it would take, even suffering for Christ, he was resolved to do so to know Him yet more.

GOD IS WORTHY

Once believers have come to the Father through His Son, they become worshipers of God. Paul writes that believers are those "who worship in the Spirit of God and glory in Christ Jesus" (Phil. 3:3). True worship is the only rightful response to God. It is recognizing that He alone is worthy to receive praise. Our whole being—mind, affections, and will—must respond with wonder to the majesty of God. As Moses recorded long ago, "You shall love the LORD your God with all your heart and with all your soul and with all your might" (Deut. 6:5). Jesus reaffirmed this fundamental priority (Matt. 22:37; Mark 12:30; Luke 10:27). God alone is worthy of our supreme affection and greatest adoration.

The word "worship" comes from an Old English word that means "worthiness." Worship means to make known the worthiness of someone or something. In this case, it is declaring to God His own worthiness. It is the proper response to recognizing the supreme worth of God. The more we grow to know God, the more we will behold His worthiness. In turn, the more we consider His worthiness, the more we will worship Him. As it was for Moses, the key for us is to behold more of His glory. Our heart cry must be, "Show me Your glory!" As we experience clearer visions of His beauty, we will worship Him more—and more.

In the time of the New Testament, the word "worthy" (Greek *axios*) was used of a tribute given to the returning Roman general as he marched into Rome after a great victory. In a triumphal procession, this conquering military commander led a march of grandeur through the streets of the Eternal City. First came the state officials and the senate. Then came the trumpeters sounding the approach of the spoils taken from the conquered land. Next came images of the conquered land and models of conquered citadels and ships. Then were ushered the captive princes and opposing generals in chains. They were to be thrown into prison and executed. Then came the lectors bearing their rods, followed by the musicians with their lyres. The priests came swinging their censers with the sweet-smelling incense burning in them.

Finally, after great anticipation, there came the mighty general himself, riding majestically in a chariot drawn by four horses. He wore a crown of laurels on his head. A purple tunic, embroidered with golden stars, was draped on his shoulders. In his hand, he held aloft an ivory scepter with the Roman eagle at its top. Over his head, a slave held the crown of Jupiter. After this display of victory, his family and his army rode in, wearing their formal military attire. Toward him came the responding shouts of triumph: *"Io triumphe!"* As the procession moved through the streets, the adoring crowds cheered loudly. The general's procession ascended the Capitoline Hill to the Temple of Jupiter as acts of worship were given to him.

In the same way, Jesus Christ has won the ultimate victory over all our enemies. He is triumphant over sin, Satan, and the world. In His ascension, He returned to heaven and was seated "at the right hand of the Majesty on high" (Heb. 1:3). As believers, we come before God to ascribe to Him His due worthiness. This great Victor has made us acceptable through the sinless life and substitutionary death of His Son, Jesus Christ. As we approach the throne of grace, we come boldly through the merit of our sin-bearing Savior and Lord. We come before God declaring the victory of Jesus over all heaven's enemies (2 Cor. 2:14; Col. 2:15). Our praise goes to the Father, who sent His Son into this world to secure our salvation.

GOD IS CAPTIVATING

In heaven, the worthiness of God is forever being pronounced by those before His throne. The Father is being praised: "Worthy are You, our Lord and our God, to receive glory and honor and power; for You created all things, and because of Your will they existed, and were created" (Rev. 4:11). This fervent praise is being lifted up to Creator God, who is worthy of the adoration being given by redeemed saints. He is receiving endless glory in recognition of the honor and power that belong to Him. He created all things *by* Himself and *for* Himself. For the whole of His marvelous works, He is being praised.

Further, Jesus Christ is being declared worthy in heaven to receive this worship:

"Worthy are You to take the book and to break its seals; for You were slain, and purchased for God with Your

262

blood men from every tribe and tongue and people and nation.

"You have made them to be a kingdom and priests to our God; and they will reign upon the earth." . . .

"Worthy is the Lamb that was slain to receive power and riches and wisdom and might and honor and glory and blessing." (Rev. 5:9–10, 12)

By virtue of His saving death on the cross, Jesus—who is coequal and coeternal with the Father—is considered worthy of this same praise. He has redeemed His people and for this, they ascribe to Him the glory He rightly deserves.

DEEPER AND HIGHER

This brings us back to where our journey began. We entered the inspired narrative of Scripture, observing how Moses sought to know more of the glory of God. His passionate cry was, "Show me Your glory!" (Ex. 33:18). God's self-revelatory response brought Moses low, with his face to the ground. This self-disclosure by God led Moses to greater worship of Him. Seeing the intrinsic glory of God led him to ascribe glory to Him, as He alone is worthy to be praised.

A greater knowledge of God should have the same effect in our own lives. The deeper we grow to know God, the higher should be our praise for Him. Jesus says, "Those who worship Him must worship in spirit and truth" (John 4:24). Learning these towering truths about God should invigorate our hearts, enabling us to soar to the heights of heaven, where God is enthroned on high. Through our study of God's glorious attributes, may the truth about Him be magnified in our minds and hearts.

Have you increased in your knowledge of God through these pages? I pray that this study has drawn you closer to Him.

Our only rightful response to this knowledge of God should be to join Moses—bowed low toward the ground, giving rightful worship to God alone.

SCRIPTURE
INDEX

ABOUT
THE AUTHOR

D r. Steven J. Lawson is president and founder of OnePassion, a ministry designed to equip biblical expositors to bring about a new reformation in the church. Dr. Lawson teaches for The Institute for Expository Preaching in cities around the world. He is a teaching fellow for Ligonier Ministries and professor of preaching at The Master's Seminary, where he is dean of the doctor of ministry program. He also serves as a member of the board at both Ligonier and The Master's Seminary. In addition, he is the executive editor for *Expositor Magazine*.

Dr. Lawson served as a pastor for thirty-four years in Arkansas and Alabama. Most recently, he was senior pastor of Christ Fellowship Baptist Church in Mobile, Ala. He is a graduate of Texas Tech University (B.B.A.), Dallas Theological Seminary (Th.M.), and Reformed Theological Seminary (D.Min.).

Dr. Lawson is the author of more than two dozen books, including *New Life in Christ, The Moment of Truth, The Kind of Preaching God Blesses, The Heroic Boldness of Martin Luther, The Gospel Focus of Charles Spurgeon, Foundations of Grace, Pillars of Grace, Famine in the Land*, verse-by-verse commentaries on Psalms and Job for the Holman Old Testament Commentary series, and *Philippians for You* in the God's Word for You series. He also serves as editor of the Long Line of Godly Men Profiles series with Reformation Trust.

Dr. Lawson's books have been translated into many languages, including Russian, Italian, Portuguese, Spanish, German, Albanian, Korean, and Indonesian. He has contributed articles to magazines and theological journals including *Tabletalk*, *Banner of Truth*, *The Master's Seminary Journal*, *The Southern Baptist Journal of Theology*, *Bibliotheca Sacra*, *Decision*, and *Discipleship Journal*.